SHORT TALKS ON MASONRY

By

JOSEPH FORT NEWTON

GW00502407

MACOY PUBLISHING & MASONIC SUPPLY COMPANY, INC.

Richmond, Virginia

Printed in the United States of America

Introduction to the Macoy Edition

The literary works of *The Reverend Joseph Fort Newton* (who departed this life on January 14, 1950) in the quarries of Freemasonry have been popular for many years. His interest in the Craft came as a boy when he heard the story of his father, Lee Newton, becoming a Mason in a military lodge. The father had been taken prisoner in Arkansas Post, and was imprisoned in a military camp at Rock Island, Illinois. Exposure to the severe climate caused him to become seriously ill. An officer of the camp, recognizing Lee Newton as a brother Mason, took him to his home and nursed him back to health. When the war was over, the officer loaned the young man enough money to return home. But for the gentle act of his Masonic brother, Lee Newton would have perished as a prisoner of war, and the world and Freemasonry would have been the poorer because there would have been no Joseph Fort Newton.

Joseph Fort Newton became a minister and was assigned to a church in Dixon, Illinois, where he joined Friendship Lodge No. 7. But it was not until he lived in Cedar Rapids, Iowa, that his deep interest in Freemasonry arose when he discovered the wealth of material in the Iowa Masonic Library and started his study of Masonic history and philosophy.

His first Masonic book, *The Builders*, has been a perennial best seller since it was first published in 1914. To many Masons, this book has been his first adventure into the world of Masonic literature.

Between the years 1923 and 1927 Brother Joseph Fort Newton, at the request of the Masonic Service Association, wrote a series of talks designed to be read at lodge meetings. They proved to be so popular that they were collected and published in book form in 1928 as *Short Talks on Masonry*. This volume also has been enjoyed for many years by several generations of Masons. The reprinting of this volume will be welcomed by a new generation of Masons seeking more light.

In this book the reader will find much food for thought on many of the fundamentals of the Craft. The clear, easy-to-read style will be found relaxing and informative. The author has an inimitable way of presenting his subject so as to appeal to both the heart and mind of the reader.

Whether one is seeking information, or inspiration, or material for a series of talks before Masonic audiences, the topics covered in this book will prove valuable. One thing which will strike home with great force is that though the material in the book was written many years ago, it has relevance in the world of today because of the universal ideals so beautifully explained by the author. Here you will find many references to the *Holy Bible*, great Masons, a lucid description of Masonic emblems, and much light on the symbolism, history, and philosophy of Freemasonry.

ALPHONSE CERZA

March, 1969

THE JUNIOR DEACON

They are very shallow people who take everything literally. A Man's life of any worth is a continual allegory, and very few eyes can see the Mystery of his life—a life like the Bible, figurative —which such people can no more make out than they can the Hebrew scriptures. Byron cuts a figure but he is not figurative: Shakespeare led a life of Allegory—his works are the comments on it. —John Keats, Letter to George Keats, Feb. 18th, 1819.

TO every Mason who knows his art, life is an Allegory, and the degrees and symbols of Masonry are the comments on it, interpreting its meaning and expounding its duties and its hopes. By the same token, a literal minded man can never know the real meaning of Masonry, any more than he can read the Bible aright, since both speak in metaphors and parables, for such as have eyes to see and ears to hear.

That is to say, Masonry is a kind of moral poetry —a practical mysticism, as some of us call it—uniting the basic truths of faith with the tasks and duties of every day, seeking to build men and make them workmen in the service of fraternal righteousness. Man has made rapid advance and sought him out many inventions; but never yet has he found a profounder philosophy of life or a wiser way of living it than has been brought down to us from a far past in the Lodges of our gentle craft of Masonry.

In our jumpy, jerky, jazzy generation, so wise in its own conceit and so tiresome in its egotism, such teaching may seem simple and quaint, if not odd and old-fashioned. No matter; it has stood the test of many generations; it has seen the rise and fall of many fads, many philosophies; it is truth learned by living, and is no more out of date than the Ten Commandments or the Multiplication Table. Some things abide, else we are adrift and astray—since, if nothing is fixed, no one would be aware of progress—and it is the part of wisdom to keep the landmarks of the life of man ever in view.

Such, at least, is the spirit and point of view of these brief talks and essays, all of them written for the Masonic Service Association of the United States in its effort to induce Masons to know more about Masonry, and to do more with it. Many of them were intended to be read, and have been read, in the Lodges of its member Jurisdictions, as a part of its educational work; and their purpose has naturally determined their form, which is untechnical and popular. They do not deal with the entire Masonic system, but only with a selection of its symbols—old, familiar, and lovely—at the same time urging the value of Masonry as an asset in the making of better men and the building of a nobler national life.

In our rapidly changing America we need the aid of every influence making for spiritual faith, moral culture, and practical patriotism, if we are to keep faith with the past. No one can rightly estimate the forces making for the moral integrity of our history and leave out of account the quiet, creative ministry of Freemasonry, alike in behalf of personal worth and social stability; and what it did in the past it will do, increasingly, let us hope, in the days that lie ahead.

—Joseph Fort Newton.

Memorial Church of St. Paul.
Overbrook, Philadelphia.

THE TRESTLEBOARD

CONTENTS

PART I – SYMBOLISM

"And give them proper instruction"

THE LETTER "G"

EVEN a stranger, entering a Masonic Lodge room, as he may do on a public occasion, must be struck by a mysterious Letter which hangs over the chair of the Master in the East. No one need tell him its meaning; it is a letter of light and tells its own story.

Yet no stranger can know its full import, much less how old it is. Indeed, few Masons are aware of all that it implies, either as symbol or history. There it shines, a focus of faith and fellowship, the emblem of the Divine Presence in the Lodge, and in the heart of each Brother composing it.

When the Lodge is opened, the mind and heart of each member should also be opened to the meaning of the great symbol, to the intent that its light and truth may become the supreme reality in our lives. When the Lodge is closed, the memory of that Divine initial and its august suggestions ought to be the last thought retained in the mind to be pondered over.

In English Lodges its meaning and use are made clearer than among us. There it shines in the center of the ceiling of the room, and the Lodge is grouped around it, rather than assembled beneath it. Below it is the checkerwork floor, symbol of the vicissitudes of life, over which hangs the white light of the Divine guidance and blessing, so much needed in our mortal journey.

Also, in the Degrees its use is more impressive. In the First and Second Degrees the symbol is visible in the roof, or sky, of the Lodge, like a benediction. In the Third Degree it is hidden, but its presence is still manifest—as every Mason knows—since the light of God is inextinguishable even in the darkest hours. In the Royal Arch it becomes visible again, but in another form and in another position, not to be named here.

Thus, in the course of the Degrees, the great Letter has descended from heaven to earth, as if to show us the deep meaning of Masonry. In other words, the purpose of initiation is to bring God and man together, and make them one. God becomes man that man may become God—a truth which lies at the heart of all religion, and most clearly revealed in our own. At bottom every form of faith is trying to lay hold of this truth, for which words were never made.

In all the old houses of initiation, as far back as we can go, some one letter of the alphabet stands out as a kind of Divine initial. In the Egyptian Mysteries it was the solar *Ra*, symbol of the spiritual Sun shining upon the mortal path. In the Greek Mysteries at Delphi it was the letter "E"—Eta—the fifth letter of the Greek alphabet, five being the symbol of man, as evidenced by the five senses.

Hence also the pentagram, or five-pointed star. In olden time Fellowcraft Masons worked in groups of five, and five Brethren now compose one of their Lodges. Plutarch tells us that in the Greek Mys-

teries the Letter Eta was made of wood in the
First Degree, of bronze in the Second Degree, and
of gold in the Third—showing the advance and refinement of the moral and spiritual nature, as well
as the higher value to the truth unfolded.

Many meanings and much history are thus gathered into the Great Letter, some of it dim and lost
to us now. In our Lodges, and in the thought of
the Craft today, the Letter G stands for Geometry
and also as the initial of our word God. Now
for one, now for the other, but nearly always for
both, since all Masonry rests upon Geometry, and
in all its lore Geometry is the way to God.

Of the first of these meanings not much needs to
be said. In the oldest Charges of the Craft, as
in its latest interpretations, it is agreed that Masonry is moral geometry. What was forefelt by
philosophers and mystics in ancient times is now revealed to us by the microscope. It is an actual fact
that Geometry is the thought-form of God in nature,
in the snowflake and in the orbits of the stars.

Since this ancient insight is confirmed by the
vision of science, in the most impressive manner
the great Letter may stand as the initial of God,
not alone by the accident of our language, but also
and much more by a faith founded in fact. There
is no longer any secret; it cannot be hid, because
it is written in the structure of things, in all the
forms which truth and beauty take.

Nor does Masonry seek to hide the fact that it
rests on God, lives in God, and seeks to lead men
to God. Everything in Masonry has reference to
God, every lesson, every lecture, from the first step

to the last degree. Without God it has no meaning, and no mission among men. It would be like
the house in the parable, built on the sand, which
the flood swept away. For Masonry, God is the
first truth and the final reality.

Yet, as a fact, Masonry rarely uses the name of
God. It uses, instead, the phrase, the Great Architect of the Universe. Of course such a phrase fits
into the symbolism of the Craft, but that is not
the only—nor, perhaps, the chief—reason why it
is used. A deep, fine feeling keeps us from using
the name of Deity too often, lest it lose some of
its awe in our minds.

It is because Masons believe in God so deeply
that they do not repeat His name frequently, and
some of us prefer the Masonic way in the matter.
Also, we love the Masonic way of teaching by in-
direction, so to speak; by influence and atmosphere.
Masonry, in its symbols and in its spirit, seeks to
bring us into the presence of God and detain us
there, and that is the wisest way.

In nothing is Masonry more deep-seeing than in
the way in which it deals with our attitude toward
God, who is both the meaning and the mystery of
life. It does not intrude, much less drive, in the
intimate and delicate things of the inner life—like
a bungler thrusting his hand into our heart-strings.

No, all that Masonry asks is that we confess our
faith in a Supreme Being. It does not require that
we analyze or define in detail our thought of God.
Few men have formulated their profoundest faith;
perhaps no man can do it, satisfactorily. It goes
deeper than the intellect, down into the instincts

and feelings, and eludes all attempts to put it into words.

Life and love, joy and sorrow, pity and pain and death, the blood in the veins of man, the milk in the breast of woman, the laughter of little children, the coming and going of days, all the old, sweet, sad, human things that make up our mortal life—these are the bases of our faith in God. Older than argument, it is deeper than debate; as old as the home, as tender as infancy and old age, as deep as love and death.

Men lived and died by faith in God long before philosophy was born, ages before theology had learned its letters. Vedic poets and penitential Psalmists were praising God on yonder side of the Pyramids. In Egypt, five thousand years ago, a poet-king sang of the unity, purity and beauty of God, celebrating His presence revealed, yet also concealed, in the order of life.

No man can put such things into words, much less into a hard and fast dogma. Masonry does not ask him to do so. All that it asks is that he tell, simply and humbly, in Whom he puts his trust in life and in death, as the source, security and sanction of moral life and spiritual faith; and that is as far as it seeks to go.

One thinks of the talk of the old Mason with the young nobleman who was an atheist, in the Tolstoi story, *War and Peace*. When the young count said with a sneer that he did not believe in God, the old Mason smiled, as a mother might smile at the silly sayings of a child. Then, in a gentle voice, the old man said:

"Yes, you do not know Him, sir. You do not know Him, that is why you are unhappy. But He is here, He is within me, He is in you, even in these scoffing words you have just uttered. If He is not, we should not be speaking of Him, sir. Whom dost thou deny?"

They were silent for a spell, as the train moved on. Something in the old man touched the Count deeply, and stirred in him a longing to see what the old man saw and know what he knew. His eyes betrayed his longing to know God, and the old man read his face and answered his unasked questions:

"Yes, He exists, but to know Him is hard. It is not attained by reason, but by life. The highest truth is like the purest dew. Could I hold in an impure vessel the pure dew and judge of its purity? Only by inner purification can we know God."

All these things—all this history and hope and yearning which defies analysis—Masonry tells us in a shining Letter which it hangs up in the Lodge. It is the wisest way; its presence is a prophecy, and its influence extends beyond our knowing, evoking one knows not what memories and meditations. Never do we see that great Letter, and think of what it implies, that we do not feel what Watts felt:

O God, our help in ages past,
　Our hope in times to come,
Our shelter from the stormy blast,
　And our eternal home.

THE LODGE

God hath made mankind one vast Brotherhood,
Himself their Master, and the world His Lodge.

OUT of an old, dark abyss a whirling fire-mist
emerged, and the world was made. Ages
afterwards a race of men began to walk about on its
surface and ask what it means. Dimly aware that
things are more than they seem to be, man sought
in the order of nature and in the depths of his own
being for a clue to the questions which haunted his
mind:

What is the world? How did it come to be?
Why does it exist? Has it a Mind, a Purpose, a
Plan? Why is man here? What is he sent to do
and be? What is life for? What is its meaning,
its duty, its hope? Is death the end? Where does
man go when he falls into a still, strange sleep, and
does not wake up?

Such faith as man won from the mystery of life,
such truth as he learned by living, he set forth in
sign and symbol, in sacred rite and ceremony, in the
Temple and the Lodge. For, next to the Home and
the House of Prayer, the Lodge is the oldest shrine
of humanity—so ancient is the idea and art of initiation, as far back as the earliest ages. Rituals,
if not the oldest records of the race, show us man
the mystic, telling himself the truth until it is real

7

and vivid, seeking to lift his life into a higher rhythm of reality.

The Men's House was the center of tribal society, the place where youth was tried, trained, and taught the secret lore of the race. Its rites were crude—often, no doubt, cruel—as all things were in the beginning; but their intent was to test men before intrusting to them treasures which had cost so much and must not be lost. Always the crowning rite of initiation was a drama of the immortal life, revealing man undefeated by death, keeping his hidden treasure—by virtue of that in him which has never accepted utter indentity with outward force and fact.

Ages later, by the same mystic insight, the art of initiation was linked with the art of building. Back of this blending of two arts lay the truth that the life of man must reproduce the law and order of the world in which he lives. So every temple became a symbol of the world—its floor the earth, its roof the heavens; and every ritual repeated the life and death of man—showing the passage of the soul through nature to Eternity. How impressive it is, uniting a truth so old that it is easily overlooked and an insight so simple that men forget its sublimity.

If not by direct historical descent, at least by spiritual affinity the same truth and insight are united in the moral art of Masonry, in which the Lodge is a symbol of the world and the ritual the drama of the life of man. Such an insight is as valid today as it was ages ago, though our idea of the shape of the world—no longer a cube, but a globe—has altered; since its moral order abides, and man must learn to live in harmony with it, building upon the will of God by His help and in His name.

The world is a Lodge in which man is to learn the Brotherly Life. So Masonry reads the mystery of the world and finds its purpose, its design, its prophecy. It is a simple faith, a profound philosophy, and a practical way of life. How to live is the one matter, and he will wander far without learning a better way than is shown us in the Lodge. Still less may one hope to find an atmosphere more gentle for the growth of the best things, or a wiser method of teaching the truth by which man is inspired and edified.

In the days of Operative Masonry, a lodge was a hut or a shed, of a temporary kind, near the place where the work was carried on. It was variously used as an office, a storeroom, or a place where the workmen ate and slept together, as we read in the Fabric Rolls of York Minster, in orders issued to the Craft in 1352. Not unnaturally, in time the name of the room came to describe the associations and meetings of the men using the lodge room; and they were called the Lodge. Hence our habit of speaking of the Fraternity itself as a Lodge, and so it is, since in its symbolic world men are built together in love.

At one time the Tracing Board, as it is called in England, was known as the "Lodge"; as when Preston tells how "the Grand Master, attended by his officers, form themselves in order round the lodge, which is placed in the center, covered with white satin." Again, in the Book of Constitutions, 1784, we read of "four tylers carrying the lodge covered with white satin"; as if it were a mystic Ark of the Covenant, as used in certain Masonic ceremonies. Such a use of the word, however, has passed away, or well nigh so, along with the practice.

For us the Lodge is the world, and some trace the word Lodge back to the Sanskrit word Loga, meaning the world. However that may be, manifestly it goes back to the days when men thought the world was square, and to live "on the square" meant to be at one with the order of the world. Also, since the lodge is "the place where Masons work," its form, position, dimension, covering and support are likewise symbolical of the conditions in which man lives, going forth to his labor until the evening, and the night cometh when no man can work. As Goethe put it in his poem:

> The Mason's ways are
> A type of Existence,
>   And his persistence
> Is as the days are
>   Of men in this world.

By the same token, if the Lodge is the world, so initiation is a symbol of our birth into it. But it is only an analogy, and may be pressed too far, as is often done, leaving it cloudy with ideas which have no place in it. For the Masonic initiation is a symbol of our birth out of the dim sense-life into a world of moral values and spiritual vision; out of the animal into the angel. Not to see that it is a moral and spiritual birth, in which the hood-winks of the flesh are removed, is to miss both its meaning and its beauty.

Back of the art and practice of initiation, in the olden time, lay a profound idea, never better told than in the Hymn of the Soul in an old book called the *Acts of Thomas*. The story is told by the Soul itself, of its descent from the house of its Father to Egypt to fetch a Pearl away. Before it left its heavenly home, its White Robe and Scarlet Tunic were removed, and it went naked into a far country in quest of a Pearl of great price, to find which all else might well be given up.

In Egypt the Soul eats of the food of the land, forgets its Father and serves the King of Egypt— forgets the Pearl, as if overcome by a deep sleep. But a Letter is sent to it by its Father, bidding it remember that it is the son of a King, and to call to mind the Pearl and the White Robe left above. The Letter flies in the likeness of an eagle. The Soul awakes, seizes the Pearl, strips off its filthy, unclean dress, and sets off eastward and homeward, guided by the light of the Letter, from Egypt, past Babylon to Maisham on the sea.

There the Soul meets the White Robe, and be-cause it only dimly remembered its fashion—for in its childhood it had left the Robe in its Father's House—the Robe became a mirror of the Soul. "All over it the instincts of knowledge were work-ing." The White Robe speaks and tells how it grew as the Soul grew, and then of itself it in-vests the Soul with that of which it had been di-vested—a perfect fit—and the Soul returns to its

Home, like the Prodigal Son in the parable of Jesus.
Thus our initiation is a return of the Soul, along
a dim, hard path, led by a Shining Letter hung up
in the Lodge; the discovery by man of who he is,
whence he came, and whose son he is.

So understood, the ritual of initiation is a drama
of the eternal life of man, of the awakening of the
soul and the building of character. For character
is built of thoughts and by thought, and the Lodge
offers both a place of quiet and purity and a method
by which the work may be carried on, isolated from
the confusion of the ordinary life. Sect and party,
creed and strife, are excluded. Not out of the
world, but separate from it, "close tyled," in a
chamber of moral imagery, and in the fellowship
of men seeking the good life, we may learn what
life is and how to live it.

Outside, angry passion and bad ambition fill
the earth with their cries. At the door of the Lodge,
vice, hate, envy, and the evil that work such havoc,
are left behind. Inside, the Faith that makes us
men is taught by old and simple symbols, and the
Moral Life becomes as real and vivid as it is lovely.
Where, in all the world, is there such another shrine
of peace and beauty where men of all ranks, creeds
and conditions are drawn together, as brothers of
one mystic tie, dedicated and devoted to the best
life!

Here, in the Lodge, in a world of the ideal made
real, we meet upon the Level and part upon the
Square, sons of one Father, brothers in one family,
united by oath and insight, and a Love which is a
Pearl of great value, seeking a truth that makes us

free and a friendship that makes us fraternal. Outside the home and the House of God there is nothing finer than this old, far embracing Lodge of ennobled humanity.

No hammers fell, nor ponderous axes rung,
Like some tall palm the mystic fabric sprung.

THE ALTAR

A MASONIC LODGE is a symbol of the world as it was thought to be in the olden time. Our ancient Brethren had a profound insight when they saw that the world is a Temple, over-hung by starry canopy by night, lighted by the journeying sun by day, wherein man goes forth to his labor on a checker-board of lights and shadows, joys and sorrows, seeking to reproduce on earth the law and order of heaven. The visible world was but a picture or reflection of the invisible, and at its center stood the Altar of sacrifice, obligation, and adoration.

While we hold a view of the world very unlike that held by our ancient Brethren—knowing it to be round, not flat and square—yet their insight is still true. The whole idea was that man, if he is to build either a House of Faith or an order of Society that is to endure, must imitate the laws and principles of the world in which he lives. That is also our dream and design; the love of it ennobles our lives; it is our labor and our worship. To fulfill it we, too, need wisdom and help from above; and so at the center of our Lodge stands the same Altar—older than all temples, as old as life itself—a focus of faith and fellowship, at once a symbol and shrine of that unseen element of

14

thought and yearning that all men are aware of
and which no one can define.

Upon this earth there is nothing more impressive
than the silence of a company of human beings
bowed together at an altar. No thoughtful man
but at some time has mused over the meaning of
this great adoring habit of our humanity, and the
wonder of it deepens the longer he ponders it. The
instinct which thus draws men together in prayer
is the strange power which has drawn together the
stones of great cathedrals, where the mystery of
God is embodied. So far as we know, man is the
only being on our planet that pauses to pray, and
the wonder of his worship tells us more about him
than any other fact. By some deep necessity of
his nature he is a seeker after God, and in moments of sadness or longing, in hours of tragedy
or terror, he lays aside his tools and looks out over
the far horizon.

The history of the Altar in the life of man is a
story more fascinating than any fiction. Whatever
else man may have been—cruel, tyrannous, or vin-
dictive—the record of his long search for God is
enough to prove that he is not wholly base, not
altogether an animal. Rites horrible, and often
bloody, may have been a part of his early ritual, but
if the history of past ages had left us nothing but
the memory of a race at prayer, it would have left
us rich. And so, following the good custom of the
men which were of old, we set up an Altar in the
Lodge, lifting up hands in prayer, moved thereto
by the ancient need and aspiration of our humanity.
Like the men who walked in the gray years agone,

our need is for the living God to hallow these our days and years, even to the last ineffable homeward sigh which men call death.

The earliest Altar was a rough, unhewn stone set up, like the stone which Jacob set up at Bethel when his dream of a ladder, on which angels were ascending and descending, turned his lonely bed into a house of God and a gate of heaven. Later, as faith became more refined, and the idea of sacrifice grew in meaning, the Altar was built of hewn stone—cubical in form—cut, carved, and often beautifully wrought, on which men lavished jewels and priceless gifts, deeming nothing too costly to adorn the place of prayer. Later still, when men erected a Temple dedicated and adorned as the House of God among men, there were two altars, one of sacrifice, and one of incense. The altar of sacrifice, where slain beasts were offered, stood in front of the Temple; the altar of incense, on which burned the fragrance of worship, stood within. Behind all was the far withdrawn Holy Place into which only the high priest might enter.

As far back as we can go the Altar was the center of human Society, and an object of peculiar sanctity by virture of that law of association by which places and things are consecrated. It was a place of refuge for the hunted or the tormented—criminals or slaves—and to drag them away from it by violence was held to be an act of sacrilege, since they were under the protection of God. At the Altar marriage rites were solemnized, and treaties made or vows taken in its presence were more holy and binding than if made elsewhere, because there man invoked God as witness. In all the religions of antiquity, and especially among the peoples who worshipped the Light, it was the usage of both priests and people to pass around the Altar, following the course of the sun—from the East, by way of the South, to the West—singing hymns of praise as a part of their worship. Their ritual was thus an allegorical picture of the truth which underlies all religion—that man must live on earth in harmony with the rhythm and movement of heaven.

From facts and hints such as these we begin to see the meaning of the Altar in Masonry, and the reason for its position in the Lodge. In English Lodges, as in the French and Scottish Rites, it stands in front of the Master in the East. In the York Rite, so called, it is placed in the center of the Lodge—more properly a little to the East of the center—about which all Masonic activities revolve. It is not simply a necessary piece of furniture, a kind of table intended to support the Holy Bible, the Square and Compasses. Alike by its existence and its situation it identifies Masonry as a religious institution, and yet its uses are not exactly the same as the offices of an Altar in a cathedral or a shrine. Here is a fact often overlooked, and we ought to get it clearly in our minds.

The position of the Altar in the Lodge is not accidental, but profoundly significant. For, while Masonry is not a religion, it is religious in its faith and basic principles, no less than in its spirit and purpose. And yet it is not a Church. Nor does it attempt to do what the Church is trying to do. If it were a Church its Altar would be in the East and its ritual would be altered accordingly. That is to say, Masonry is not a Religion, much less a sect, but a Worship in which all men can unite, because it does not undertake to explain, or dogmatically to settle in detail, those issues by which men are divided. Beyond the primary, fundamental facts of faith it does not go. With the philosophy of those facts, and the differences and disputes growing out of them, it has not to do. In short, the position of the Altar in the Lodge is a symbol of what Masonry believes the Altar should be in actual life, a center of union and fellowship, and not a cause of division, as is now so often the case. It does not seek uniformity of opinion, but it does seek fraternity of spirit, leaving each one free to fashion his own philosophy of ultimate truth. As we may read in the Constitutions of 1723:

"A Mason is obliged, by his Tenure, to obey the moral Law; and if he rightly understands the Art, he will never be a stupid Atheist, nor an irreligious Libertine. But though in ancient Times Masons were charged in every Country to be of the Religion of that Country or Nation, whatever it was, yet 'tis now thought more expedient only to oblige them to that Religion in which all Men agree, leaving their particular Opinions to themselves; that is, to be good Men and true, or Men of Honour and Honesty, by whatever Denominations or Persuasions they may be distinguished; whereby Masonry becomes the Center of Union, and the Means of conciliating true Friendship among Persons that must have remained at a perpetual Distance."

Surely those are memorable words, a Magna Charta of friendship and fraternity. Masonry goes hand in hand with religion until religion enters the field of sectarian feud, and there it stops; because Masonry seeks to unite men, not to divide them. Here, then, is the meaning of the Masonic Altar and its position in the Lodge. It is, first of all, an Altar of faith—the deep, eternal faith which underlies all creeds and over-arches all sects; faith in God, in the moral law, and in the life everlasting. Faith in God is the corner-stone and the key-stone of Freemasonry. It is the first truth and the last, the truth that makes all other truths true, without which life is a riddle and fraternity a futility. For, apart from God the Father, our dream of the Brotherhood of Man is as vain as all the vain things proclaimed of Solomon—a fiction having no basis or hope in fact.

At the same time, the Altar of Masonry is an Altar of Freedom—not freedom *from* faith, but freedom *of* faith. Beyond the fact of the reality of God it does not go, allowing every man to think of God according to his experience of life and his vision of truth. It does not define God, much less dogmatically determine how and what men shall think or believe about God. There dispute and division begin. As a matter of fact, Masonry is not speculative at all, but operative, or rather co-operative. While all its teaching implies the Fatherhood of God, yet its ritual does not actually affirm that truth, still less make it a test of fellowship. Behind this silence lies a deep and wise reason. Only by the practice of Brotherhood do men realize the Divine Fatherhood, as a true-hearted poet has written:

"No man could tell me what my soul might be;
  I sought for God, and He eluded me;
  I sought my Brother out, and found all three."

Hear one fact more, and the meaning of the Masonic Altar will be plain. Often one enters a great Church, like Westminster Abbey, and finds it empty, or only a few people in the pews here and there, praying or in deep thought. They are sitting quietly, each without reference to others, seeking an opportunity for the soul to be alone, to communicate with mysteries greater than itself, and find healing for the bruisings of life. But no one ever goes to a Masonic Altar alone. No one bows before it at all except when the Lodge is open and in the presence of his Brethren. It is an Altar of Fellowship, as if to teach us that no man can learn the truth for another, and no man can learn it alone. Masonry brings men together in mutual respect, sympathy, and good will, that we may learn in love the truth that is hidden by apathy and lost by hate.

For the rest, let us never forget—what has been so often and so sadly forgotten—that the most sacred Altar on earth is the soul of man—your soul and mine; and that the Temple and its ritual are not ends in themselves, but beautiful means to the end that every human heart may be a sanctuary of faith, a shrine of love, an altar of purity, pity, and unconquerable hope. One thinks of a lovely

little poem by George Herbert, called "The Altar,"
in which a tender heart is opened wide.

A broken altar, Lord, The servant reares,
Made of a heart, and cemented with teares:
 Whose parts are as Thy hand did frame;
 No workman's tool hath touched the same.
    A heart alone
    Is such a stone,
    As nothing but
    Thy power doth cut.
    Wherefore each part
    Of my hard heart
    Meets in this frame
    To praise Thy name.
 That if I chance to hold my peace,
 These stones to praise Thee may not cease.
O let Thy blessed sacrifice be mine,
And sanctify this altar to be Thine.

THE HOLY BIBLE

UPON the Altar of every Masonic Lodge, supporting the Square and Compasses, lies the Holy Bible. The old, familiar Book, so beloved by so many generations, is our Volume of Sacred Law and a Great Light in Masonry. The Bible opens when the Lodge opens: it closes when the Lodge closes. No Lodge can transact its own business, much less initiate candidates into its mysteries, unless the Book of Holy Law lies open upon its Altar. Thus the book of the Will of God rules the Lodge in its labors, as the Sun rules the day, making its work a worship.

The history of the Bible in the life and symbolism of Masonry is a story too long to recite here. Nor can any one tell it as we should like to know it. Just when, where, and by whom the teaching and imagery of the Bible were wrought into Freemasonry, no one can tell. Anyone can have his theory, but no one can be dogmatic. As the Craft labored in the service of the Church during the cathedral-building period, it is not difficult to account for the Biblical coloring of its thought, even in days when the Bible was not widely distributed, and before the discovery of printing. Anyway, we can take such facts as we are able to find, leaving further research to learn further truth.

The Bible is mentioned in some of the old Manuscripts of the Craft long before the revival of Masonry in 1717, as the book upon which the covenant, or oath, of a Mason was taken; but it is not referred to as a Great Light. For example, in the Harleian Manuscript, dated about 1600, the obligation of an initiate closes with the words: "So help me God, and the holy contents of this book." In the old Ritual, of which a copy from the Royal Library in Berlin is given by Krause, there is no mention of the Bible as one of the Lights. It was in England, due largely to the influence of Preston and his fellow workmen, that the Bible came to its place of honor in the Lodge. At any rate, in the rituals of about 1760 it is described as one of the three Great Lights.

No Mason needs to be told what a great place the Bible has in the Masonry of our day. It is central, sovereign, supreme, a master light of all our seeing. From the Altar it pours forth upon the East, the West, and the South its white light of spiritual vision, moral law, and immortal hope. Almost every name found in our ceremonies is a Biblical name, and students have traced about seventy-five references to the Bible in the Ritual of the Craft. But more important than direct references is the fact that the spirit of the Bible, its faith, its attitude toward life, pervades Masonry, like a rhythm or a fragrance. As soon as an initiate enters the Lodge, he hears the words of the Bible recited as an accompaniment to his advance toward the light. Upon the Bible every Mason takes solemn vows of loyalty, of chastity and charity, pledg-

ing himself to the practice of the Brotherly Life.
Then as he moves forward from one degree to
another, the imagery of the Bible becomes familiar
and eloquent, and its music sings its way into his
heart.

Nor is it strange that it should be so. As faith
in God is the corner-stone of the Craft, so, naturally, the book which tells us the purest truth about
God is its altar-light. The Temple of King Solomon, about which the history, legends, and symbolism of the Craft are woven, was the tallest temple
of the ancient world, not in the grandeur of its
architecture but in the greatest of the truths for
which it stood. In the midst of ignorant idolatries
and debasing superstitions the Temple on Mount
Moriah stood for the Unity, Righteousness, and
Spirituality of God. Upon no other foundation
can men build with any sense of security and per-
manence when the winds blow and the floods de-
scend. But the Bible is not simply a foundation
rock; it is also a quarry in which we find the truths
that make us men. As in the old ages of geology
rays of sunlight were stored up in vast beds of coal,
for the uses of man, so in this old book the light of
moral truth is stored to light the mind and warm
the heart of man.

Alas, there has been more dispute about the
Bible than about any other book, making for
schism, dividing men into sects. But Masonry
knows a certain secret, almost too simple to be
found out, whereby it avoids both intolerance and
sectarianism. It is essentially religious, but it is
not dogmatic. The fact that the Bible lies open

upon its Altar means that man must have some Divine revelation—must seek for a light higher than human to guide and govern him. But it lays down no hard and fast dogma on the subject of revelation. It attempts no detailed interpretation of the Bible. The great Book lies open upon its Altar, and is open for all to read, open for each to interpret for himself. The tie by which our Craft is united is strong, but it allows the utmost liberty of faith and thought. It unites men, not upon a creed bristling with debated issues, but upon the broad, simple truth which underlies all creeds and over-arches all sects—faith in God, the wise Master Builder, for whom and with whom man must work.

Herein our gentle Craft is truly wise, and its wisdom was never more needed than today, when the churches are divided and torn by angry debate. However religious teachers may differ in their doctrines, in the Lodge they meet with mutual respect and good will. At the Altar of Masonry they learn not only toleration, but appreciation. In its air of kindly fellowship, man to man, they discover that the things they have in common are greater than the things that divide. It is the glory of Masonry to teach Unity in essentials, Liberty in details, Charity in all things; and by this sign its spirit must at last prevail. It is the beautiful secret of Masonry that all just men, all devout men, all righteous men are everywhere of one religion, and it seeks to remove the hoodwinks of prejudice and intolerance so that they may recognize each other and work together in the doing of good.

Like everything else in Masonry, the Bible, so

rich in symbolism, is itself a symbol—that is, a part taken for the whole. It is a symbol of the Book of Truth, the Scroll of Faith, the Record of the Will of God as man has learned it in the midst of the years—the perpetual revelation of Himself which God has made, and is making, to mankind in every age and land. Thus, by the very honor which Masonry pays to the Bible, it teaches us to revere every Book of Faith in which men find help for today and hope for the morrow. For that reason, in a Lodge consisting entirely of Jews, the Old Testament alone may be placed upon the Altar, and in a Lodge in the land of Mohammed the Koran may be used. Whether it be the Gospels of the Christian, the Book of Law of the Hebrew, the Koran of the Mussulman, or the Vedas of the Hindu, it everywhere Masonically conveys the same idea—symbolizing the Will of God revealed to man, taking such faith and vision as he has found into a great fellowship of the seekers and finders of the truth, which is larger than all creeds and dogmas.

Thus Masonry invites to its Altar men of all faiths, knowing that, if they use different names for "the Nameless One of an hundred names," they are yet praying to the one God and Father of all; knowing, also, that while they read different volumes, they are in fact reading the same vast Book of the Faith of Man as revealed in the struggle and tragedy of the race in its quest of God. So that, great and noble as the Bible is, Masonry sees it as a symbol of that eternal, ever-unfolding Book of the Will of God which Lowell described in memorable lines:

Slowly the Bible of the race is writ,
    And not on paper leaves nor leaves of stone;
Each age, each kindred, adds a verse to it,
    Texts of despair or hope, of joy or moan.
While swings the sea, while mists the mountain
        shroud,
    While thunder's surges burst on cliffs of cloud,
Still at the Prophets' feet the nations sit.

None the less, while we honor every Book of
Faith in which have been recorded the way and
will of God, with us the Bible is supreme, at once
the mother-book of our literature and the master-
book of the Lodge. Its truth is inwrought in the
fiber of our being, with whatsoever else of the good
and the true which the past has given us. Its spirit
stirs our hearts, like a sweet habit of the blood; its
light follows all our way, showing us the meaning
and worth of life. Its very words have in them
memories, echoes and overtones of voices long since
hushed, and its scenery is interwoven with the holiest associations of our lives. Our fathers and
mothers read it, finding in it their final reasons for
living faithfully and nobly, and it is thus a part of
the ritual of the Lodge and the ritual of life.

Every Mason ought not only to honor the Bible
as a great Light of the Craft; he ought to read it,
live with it, love it, lay its truth to heart and learn
what it means to be a man. There is something in
the old Book which, if it gets into a man, makes
him both gentle and strong, faithful and free, obedient and tolerant, adding to his knowledge, virtue,
patience, temperance, self-control, brotherly love,

and pity. The Bible is as high as the sky and as deep as the grave; its two great characters are God and the Soul, and the story of their eternal life together is its everlasting romance. It is the most human of books, telling us the half-forgotten secrets of our own hearts, our sins, our sorrows, our doubts, our hopes. It is the most Divine of books, telling us that God has made us for Himself, and that our hearts will be restless, unhappy and lonely until we learn to rest in Him whose will is our peace.

"He hath showed thee, O man, what is good; and what doth the Lord require of thee, but to do justly, to love mercy, and to walk humbly with thy God."

"Thou shalt love the Lord thy God with all thy heart, and with all thy soul, and with all thy strength, and with all thy mind; and thy neighbor as thyself."

"Therefore all things whatsoever ye would that men should do to you, do ye even so to them; for this is the law and the prophets."

"Pure religion and undefiled before God and the Father is this, To visit the fatherless and widows in their affliction, and to keep himself unspotted from the world."

"For we know that if our earthly house of this tabernacle were dissolved, we have a building of God, a house not made with hands, eternal in the heavens."

THE SQUARE

THE Holy Bible lies open upon the Altar of Masonry, and upon the Bible lie the Square and Compasses. They are the three Great Lights of the Lodge, at once its Divine warrant and its chief working tools. They are symbols of Revelation, Righteousness, and Redemption, teaching us that by walking in the light of Truth, and obeying the law of Right, the Divine in man wins victory over the earthly. It is the philosophy of Life in epitome, set forth in simple symbols. How to live is the one important matter, and he will seek far without finding a wiser way than that shown us by the Great Lights of the Lodge.

The Square and Compasses are the oldest, the simplest, and the most universal symbols of Masonry. All the world over, whether as a sign on a building, or a badge worn by a Brother, even the profane know them to be emblems of our ancient Craft. Some years ago, when a business firm tried to adopt the Square and Compasses as a trademark, the Patent Office refused permission, on the ground, as the decision said, that "there can be no doubt that this device, so commonly worn and employed by Masons, has an established mystic significance, universally recognized as existing; whether comprehended by all or not, is not material to this issue." They belong to us, alike by the associations of history and the tongue of common report.

Nearly everywhere in our Ritual, as in the public mind, the Square and Compasses are seen together. If not interlocked, they are seldom far apart, and the one suggests the other. And that is as it should be, because the things they symbolize are inter-woven. In the old days when the earth was thought to be flat and square, the Square was an emblem of the Earth, and later, of the earthly element in man. As the sky is an arc or a circle, the imple-ment which describes a Circle became the symbol of the heavenly, or skyey spirit in man. Thus the tools of the builder became the emblems of the thoughts of the thinker; and nothing in Masonry is more impressive than the slow elevation of the Compasses above the Square in the progress of the degrees. The whole meaning and task of life is there, for such as have eyes to see.

Let us separate the Square from the Compasses and study it alone, the better to see its further meaning and use. There is no need to say that the Square we have in mind is not a Cube, which has four equal sides and angles, deemed by the Greeks a figure of perfection. Nor is it the square of the carpenter, one leg of which is longer than the other, with inches marked for measuring. It is a small, plain Square, unmarked and with legs of equal length, a simple try-square used for testing the accuracy of angles, and the precision with which stones are cut. Since the try-square was used to prove that angles were right, it naturally became an

emblem of accuracy, integrity, rightness. As stones
are cut to fit into a building, so our acts and
thoughts are built together into a structure of Character, badly or firmly, and must be tested by a moral
standard of which the simple try-square is a symbol.

So, among Speculative Masons, the tiny try-
square has always been a symbol of morality, of
the basic rightness which must be the test of every
act and the foundation of character and society.
From the beginning of the Revival in 1717 this was
made plain in the teaching of Masonry, by the fact
that the Holy Bible was placed upon the Altar,
along with the Square and Compasses. In one of
the earliest catechisms of the Craft, dated 1725, the
question is asked: "How many make a lodge?"
The answer is specific and unmistakable: "God
and the square, with five or seven right or perfect
Masons." God and the Square, Religion and Morality, must be present in every lodge as its ruling
Lights, or it fails of being a just and truly consti-
tuted lodge. In all lands, in all rites where Masonry is true to itself, the Square is a symbol of
righteousness, and is applied in the light of faith
in God.

God and the Square—it is necessary to keep the
two together in our day, because the tendency of
the time is to separate them. The idea in vogue
today is that morality is enough, and that faith in
God—if there be a God—may or may not be important. Some very able men of the Craft insist
that we make the teaching of Masonry too religious.
Whereas, as all history shows, if faith in God grows
dim, morality becomes a mere custom, if not a cob-

web, to be thrown off lightly. It is not rooted in reality, and so lacks authority and sanction. Such an idea, such a spirit—so wide-spread in our time, and finding so many able and plausible advocates—strikes at the foundations, not only of Masonry, but of all ordered and advancing social life. Once let men come to think that morality is a human invention, and not a part of the order of the world, and the moral law will lose both its meaning and its power, as it has for so many in our generation. Far wiser was the old book entitled *All in All and the Same Forever,* by John Davies, and dated 1607, though written by a non-Mason, when it read the reality and nature of God in this manner: "Yet I this form of formless Deity drew by the Square and Compasses of our Creed."

For, inevitably, a society without standards will be a society without stability, and it will one day go down. Not only nations, but whole civilizations have perished in the past, for lack of righteousness. History speaks plainly in this matter, and we dare not disregard it. Hence the importance attached to the Square of Virtue, and the reason why Masons call it the great symbol of their Craft. It is a symbol of that moral law upon which human life must rest if it is to stand. A man may build a house in any way he likes, but if he expects it to stand and be his home, he must adjust his structure to the laws and forces that rule in the material realm. Just so, unless we live in obedience to the moral laws which God has written in the order of things, our lives will fall and end in wreck. When a young man forgets the simple Law of the Square, it does not need a prophet to forsee what the result will be. It is like a problem in geometry.

Such has been the meaning of the Square as far back as we can go. Long before our era we find the Square teaching the same lesson which it teaches us today. In one of the old books of China, called *The Great Learning,* which has been dated in the fifth century before Christ, we read that a man should not do unto others what he would not have them do unto him; and the writer adds, "this is called the principle of acting on the square." There it is, recorded long, long ago. The greatest philosopher has found nothing more profound, and the oldest man in his ripe wisdom has learned nothing more true. Even Jesus only altered it from the negative to the positive form in His Golden Rule. So, everywhere, in our Craft and outside, the Square has taught its simple truth which does not grow old. The Deputy Provincial Grand Master of North and East Yorkshire recovered a very curious relic, in the form of an old brass Square found under the foundation of an ancient bridge near Limerick, in 1830. On it was inscribed the date, 1517, and the following words:

> "Strive to live with love and care
> Upon the Level, by the Square."

How simple and beautiful it is, revealing the oldest wisdom man has learned and the very genius of our Craft. In fact and truth, the Square rules the Mason as well as the lodge in which he labors. As soon as he enters a lodge, the candidate walks with square steps round the square pavement of a rectangular lodge. All during the ceremony his attitude keeps him in mind of the same symbol, as if to fashion his life after its form. When he is brought to light, he beholds the Square upon the Altar, and at the same time sees that it is worn by the Master of the lodge, as the emblem of his office. In the north-east corner he is shown the perfect Ashlar, and told that it is the type of a finished Mason, who must be a Square-Man in thought and conduct, in word and act. With every art of emphasis the Ritual writes this lesson in our hearts, and if we forget this first truth the Lost Word will remain forever lost, though we journey to the ends of the earth, in quest of it.

For Masonry is not simply a Ritual; it is a way of living. It offers us a plan, a method, a faith by which we may build our days and years into a character so strong and true that nothing, not even death, can destroy it. Each of us has in his own heart a little try-square called Conscience, by which to test each thought and deed and word, whether it be true or false. By as much as a man honestly applies that test in his own heart, and in his relations with his fellows, by so much will his life be happy, stable, and true. Long ago the question was asked and answered: "Lord, who shall abide in thy tabernacle? He that walketh uprightly, and worketh righteousness, and speaketh the truth in his heart." It is the first obligation of a Mason to be on the Square, in all his duties and dealings with his fellow men, and if he fails there he cannot win anywhere. Let one of our poets sum it all up:

It matters not whate'er your lot
  Or what your task may be,
One duty there remains for you,
  One duty stands for me.
Be you a doctor skilled and wise,
  Or do your work for wage,
A laborer upon the street,
  An artist on the stage;
One glory still awaits for you,
  One honor that is fair,
To have men say as you pass by:
  "That fellow's on the square."

Ah, here's a phrase that stands for much,
  'Tis good old English, too;
It means that men have confidence
  In everything you do.
It means that what you have you've earned,
  And that you've done your best,
And when you go to sleep at night
  Untroubled you may rest.
It means that conscience is your guide,
  And honor is your care;
There is no greater praise than this:
  "That fellow's on the square."

And when I die I would not wish
  A lengthy epitaph;
I do not want a headstone large,
  Carved with fulsome chaff.
Pick out no single deed of mine,
  If such a deed there be,
To 'grave upon my monument,
  For those who come to see.
Just this one phrase of all I choose,
  To show my life was fair:
"Here sleepeth now a fellow who
  Was always on the square."

THE COMPASSES

IN our study of the Square we saw that it is nearly
always linked with the Compasses, and these
old emblems, joined with the Holy Bible, are the
Great Lights of the Craft. If the lodge is an "oblong square" and built upon the Square (as the
earth was thought to be in olden time), over it
arches the Sky, which is a circle. Thus Earth and
Heaven are brought together in the lodge—the
earth where man goes forth to his labor, and the
heaven to which he aspires. In other words, the
light of Revelation and the law of Nature are like
the two points of the Compasses within which our
life is set under a canopy of Sun and Stars.

No symbolism can be more simple, more profound, more universal, and it becomes more wonderful the longer one ponders it. Indeed, if Masonry
is in any sense a religion, it is Universe Religion, in
which all men can unite. Its principles are as wide
as the world, as high as the sky. Nature and Revelation blend in its teaching; its morality is rooted
in the order of the world, and its roof is the blue
vault above. The lodge, as we are apt to forget, is
always open to the sky, whence come those influences which exalt and enoble the life of man.
Symbolically, at least, it has no rafters but the arch-
ing heavens to which, as sparks ascending seek the

sun, our life and labor tend. Of the heavenly side of Masonry the Compasses are the symbol, and they are perhaps the most spiritual of our working tools.

As has been said, the Square and Compasses are nearly always together, and that is true as far back as we can go. In the sixth book of the philosophy of Mencius, in China, we find these words: "A Master Mason, in teaching Apprentices, makes use of the compasses and the square. Ye who are engaged in the pursuit of wisdom must also make use of the compass and the square." Note the order of the words: the Compass has first place, as it should have to a Master Mason. In the oldest classic of China, *The Book of History*, dating back two thousand years before our era, we find the Compasses employed without the Square: "Ye officers of the Government, apply the Compasses." Even in that far off time these symbols had the same meaning they have for us today, and they seem to have been interpreted in the same way.

While in the order of the lodge the Square is first, in point of truth it is not the first in order. The Square rests upon the Compasses before the Compasses rest upon the Square. That is to say, just as a perfect square is a figure that can be drawn only within a circle or about a circle, so the earthly life of man moves and is built within the Circle of Divine life and law and love which surrounds, sustains, and explains it. In the Ritual of the lodge we see man, hoodwinked by the senses, slowly groping his way out of darkness, seeking the light of morality and reason. But he does so by the aid of inspiration from above, else he would live untroubled by a spark. Some deep need, some dim desire brought him to the door of the lodge, in quest of a better life and a clearer vision. Vague gleams, impulses, intimations reached him in the night of Nature, and he set forth and, finding a friendly hand to help, knocked at the door of the House of Light.

As an Apprentice a man is, symbolically, in a crude, natural state, his divine life covered and ruled by his earthly nature. As a Fellowcraft he has made one step toward liberty and light, and the nobler elements in him are struggling to rise above and control his lower, lesser nature. In the sublime Degree of a Master Mason—far more sublime than we yet realize—by human love, by the discipline of tragedy, and still more by Divine help the divine in him has subjugated the earthly, and he stands forth strong, free, and fearless, ready to raise stone upon stone until naught is wanting. If we examine with care the relative positions of the Square and Compasses as he advanced through the Degrees, we learn a parable and a prophecy of what the Compasses mean in the life of a Mason.

Here, too, we learn what the old philosopher of China meant when he urged Officers of the Government to "apply the Compasses," since only men who have mastered themselves can really lead or rule others. Let us now study the Compasses apart from the Square, and try to discover what they have to teach us. There is no more practical lesson in Masonry and it behooves us to learn it and lay it to heart. As the light of the Holy Bible reveals our relation and duty to God, and the Square instructs us in our duties to our Brother and neighbor, so the Compasses teach us the obligation which we owe to ourselves. What that obligation is needs to be made plain: it is the primary, imperative, everyday duty of circumscribing our passions, and keeping our desires within due bounds. As Most Excellent King Solomon said long ago, "better is he that ruleth his spirit than he that taketh a city."

In short, it is the old triad, without which character loses its symmetry, and life may easily end in chaos and confusion. It has been put in many ways, but never better than in the three great words: self-knowledge, self-reverence, self-control; and we cannot lose any one of the three and keep the other two. To know ourselves, our strength, our weakness, our limitations, is the first principle of wisdom, and a security against many a pitfall and blunder. Lacking such knowledge, or disregarding it, a man goes too far, loses control of himself, and by that very fact loses, in some measure, the self-respect which is the corner stone of character. If he loses respect for himself, he does not long keep his respect for others, and goes down the road to destruction, like a star out of orbit, or a car into the ditch.

The old Greeks put the same truth into a trinity of maxims: "Know thyself; in nothing too much; think as a mortal"; and it made them masters of the art of life and the life of art. Hence their wise Doctrine of the Limit, as a basic idea both of life and of thought, and their worship of the God of Bounds, of which the Compasses are a symbol. It is the wonder of our human life that we belong to the limited and to the unlimited. Hemmed in, hedged about, restricted, we long for a liberty without rule or limit. Yet limitless liberty is anarchy and slavery. As in the great word of Burke, "It is ordained in the eternal constitution of things, that a man of intemperate passions cannot be free; his passions forge their fetters." Liberty rests upon law. The wise man is he who takes full account of both, who knows how, at all points, to qualify the one by the other, as the Compasses, if he uses them aright, will teach him how to do.

Much of our life is ruled for us whether we will or not. The laws of nature throw about us their restraining bands, and there is no place where their writ does not run. The laws of the land make us aware that our liberty is limited by the equal rights and liberties of others. Our neighbor, too, if we fail to act toward him squarely may be trusted to look after his own rights. Custom, habit, and the pressure of public opinion are impalpable restraining forces which we dare not altogether defy. They are so many roads from which our passions and appetites stray at our peril. But there are other regions of life where personality has free play, and they are the places where most of our joy and sorrow lies. It is in the realm of desire, emotion, motive, in the inner life where we are freest and most alone, that we need a wise and faithful use of the Compasses.

How to use the Compasses is one of the finest of all arts, asking for the highest skill of a Master Mason. If he is properly instructed, he will rest one point on the innermost center of his being, and

with the other draw a circle beyond which he will
not go, until he is ready and able to go farther.
Against the littleness of his knowledge he will set
the depths of his desire to know, against the brevity
of his earthly life the reach of his spiritual hope.
Within a wise limit he will live and labor and grow,
and when he reaches the outer rim of the circle he
will draw another, and attain to a full-orbed life,
balanced, beautiful, and finely poised. No wise
man dare forget the maxim, "In nothing too much,"
for there are situations where a word too much, a
step too far, means disaster. If he has a quick
tongue, a hot temper, a dark mood, he will apply
the Compasses, shut his weakness within the circle
of his strength, and control it.

Strangely enough, even a virtue, if unrestrained
and left to itself, may actually become a vice.
Praise, if pushed too far, becomes flattery. Love
often ends in a soft sentimentalism, flabby and
foolish. Faith, if carried to the extreme by the will
to believe, ends in over-belief and superstition. It
is the Compasses that help us to keep our balance,
in obedience to the other Greek maxim: "Think as
a mortal"—that is, remember the limits of human
thought. An old mystic said that God is a circle
whose center is everywhere, and its circumference
nowhere. But such an idea is all a blur. Our minds
can neither grasp nor hold it. Even in our thought
about God we must draw a circle enclosing so much
of His nature as we can grasp and realize, enlarging
the circle as our experience and thought and vision
expand. Many a man loses all truth in his impatient effort to reach final truth. It is the man who

fancies that he has found the only truth, the whole truth, and nothing but the truth, and who seeks to impose his dogma upon others, who becomes the bigot, the fanatic, the persecutor.

Here, too, we must apply the Compasses, if we would have our faith fulfill itself in fellowship. Now we know in part—a small part, it may be, but it is real as far as it goes—though it be as one who sees in a glass darkly. The promise is that if we are worthy and well qualified, we shall see God face to face and know even as we are known. But God is so great, so far beyond my mind and yours, that if we are to know Him at all truly, we must know Him together, in fellowship and fraternity. And so the Poet-Mason was right when he wrote:

> "He drew a circle that shut me out,
> Heretic, rebel, a thing to flout;
> But love and I had the wit to win,
> We drew a circle that took him in."

THE LEVEL AND PLUMB

L IKE the Square and the Compasses, the Level and the Plumb are nearly always united in our Ritual. They really belong together, as much in moral teaching as in practical building. The one is used to lay horizontals, the other to try perpendiculars, and their use suggests their symbolism. By reason of their use, both are special working tools of the Fellowcraft, along with the Square; and they are also worn as jewels by two of the principal officers of the lodge.

Among the Craft Masons of olden time the actual work of building was done by Fellowcrafts, using materials gathered and rough hewn by Apprentices, all working under the guidance of the Master. In our symbolism, as the Apprentice is youth, so the Fellowcraft is manhood, the time when the actual work of life must be done on the Level, by the Plumb and Square. Next to the Square and Compasses, the Level and Plumb are among the noblest and simplest symbols of the Craft, and their meaning is so plain that it hardly needs to be pointed out. Yet they are so important, in use and meaning, that they might almost be numbered among the Lesser Lights of the lodge.

The Level, so the newly made Mason is taught, is for the purpose of proving horizontals. An

English writer finds a lesson in the structure of the Level, in the fact that we know that a surface is level when the fluid is poised and at rest. From this use of the Level he bids us seek to attain a peaceful, balanced poise of mind, undisturbed by the passions which upset and sway us one way or the other. It is a counsel of perfection, he admits, but he insists that one of the best services of Masonry is to keep before us high ideals, and, what is more, a constantly receding ideal, otherwise we should tire of it.

Of course, the great meaning of the Level is that it teaches equality, and that is a truth that needs to be carefully understood. There is no little confusion of mind about it. Our Declaration of American Independence tells us that all men are "created equal," but not many have tried to think out what the words really mean. With most of us it is a vague sentiment, a glittering generality born of the fact that all are made of the same dust, are sharers of the common human lot, moved by the same great faiths and fears, hopes and loves—walking on the Level of time until Death, by its grim democracy, erases all distinctions and reduces all to the same level.

Anyone who faces the facts knows well enough that all men are not equal, either by nature or by grace. Our humanity resembles the surface of the natural world in its hills and valleys. Men are very unequal in physical power, in mental ability, in moral quality. No two men are equal; no two are alike. One man towers above his fellows, as a mountain above the hills. Some can do what others can never do. Some have five talents, some two, and some but one. A genius can do with effortless ease what it is futile for others to attempt, and a poet may be unequal to a hod-carrier in strength and sagacity. When there is inequality of gift it is idle to talk of equality of opportunity, no matter how fine the phrase may sound. It does not exist.

By no glib theory can humanity be reduced to a dead level. The iron wrinkles of fact are stubborn realities. Manifestly it is better to have it so, because it would make a dull world if all men were equal in a literal sense. As it is, wherein one lacks another excels, and men are drawn together by the fact that they are unequal and unlike. The world has different tasks demanding different powers, brains to devise, seers to see, hands to execute, prophets to lead. We need poets to inspire, scientists to teach, pioneers to blaze the path into new lands. No doubt this was what Goethe meant when he said that it takes all men to make one man, and the work of each is the glory of all.

What, then, is the equality of which the Level is the symbol? Clearly it is not identity, or even similarity of gift and endowment. No, it is something better; it is the equal right of each man to the full use and development of such power as he has, whatever it may be, unhindered by injustice or oppression. As our Declaration of Independence puts it, every man has an equal and inalienable right to "life, liberty and the pursuit of happiness," with due regard for the rights of others in the same quest. Or, as a famous slogan summed it up: "Equal rights for all; special privileges to none!" That is to say, before the law every man has an equal right to equal justice, as before God, in whose presence all men are one in their littleness, each receives equally and impartially the blessing of the Eternal Love, even as the sun shines and the rain falls on all with equal benediction.

Albert Pike, and with him many others, have gone so far as to say that Masonry was the first apostle of equality in the true sense. One thing we do know: Freemasonry presided over the birth of our Republic, and by the skill of its leaders wrote its basic truth, of which the Level is the symbol, into the organic law of this land. The War for Independence, and the fight for constitutional liberty, might have had another issue but for the fact that our leaders were held together by a mystic tie of obligation, vowed to the service of the rights of man. Even Thomas Paine, who was not a Mason, wrote an essay in honor of an Order which stood for government without tyranny and religion without superstition—two principles which belong together, like the Level and the Plumb. Thus, by all that is sacred both in our Country and our Craft, we are pledged to guard, defend, and practice the truth taught by the Level.

But it is in the free and friendly air of a lodge of Masons, about an altar of obligation and prayer, that the principle of equality finds its most perfect and beautiful expression. There, upon the Level, the symbol of equality, rich and poor, high and low, prince and plain citizen—men of diverse creeds, parties, interests, and occupations—meet in mutual respect and real regard, forgetting all differences of rank and station, and united for the highest good of all. "We meet upon the Level and part upon the Square"; titles, ranks, riches, do not pass the Inner Guard; and the humblest brother is held in sacred regard, equally with the brother who has attained the highest round of the wheel of fortune.

Every man in the lodge is equally concerned in the building of the Temple, and each has his work to do. Because the task demands different gifts and powers, all are equally necessary to the work, the architect who draws the plans, the Apprentice who carries stones or shapes them with chisel and gavel, the Fellowcraft who polishes and deposits them in the wall, and the officers who marshal the workmen, guide their labor, and pay their wages. Every one is equal to every other so long as he does good work, true work, square work. None but is necessary to the erection of the edifice; none but receives the honor of the Craft; and all together know the joy of seeing the Temple slowly rising in the midst of their labors. Thus Masonry lifts men to a high level, making each a fellow-worker in a great enterprise, and if it is the best brotherhood it is because it is a brotherhood of the best.

II

The Plumb is a symbol so simple that it needs no exposition. As the Level teaches unity in diversity and equality in difference, so the Plumb is a symbol of rectitude of conduct, integrity of life, and that uprightness of moral character which makes a good and just man. In the art of building accuracy is integrity, and if a wall be not exactly perpendicular, as tested by the Plumb-line, it is weak and may fall, or else endanger the strength and stability of the whole. Just so, though we meet upon a Level, we must each build an upright character, by the test of the Plumb, or we weaken the Fraternity we seek to serve and imperil its strength and standing in the community.

As a workman dare not deviate by the breadth of a hair to the right or to the left if his wall is to be strong and his arch stable, so Masons must walk erect and live upright lives. What is meant by an upright life each of us knows, but it has never been better described than in the 15th Psalm, which may be called the religion of a gentleman and the design upon the Trestleboard of every Mason:

"Lord, who shall abide in Thy tabernacle? Who shall dwell in Thy holy hill? He that walketh uprightly, and worketh righteousness, and speaketh the truth in his heart. He that backbiteth not with his tongue, nor doeth evil to his neighbor, nor taketh up a reproach against his neighbor. In whose eyes a vile person is contemned; but he honoreth them that fear the Lord. He that sweareth to his own hurt, and changeth not. He that putteth not out his money to usury, nor taketh reward against the innocent. He that doeth these things shall never be moved."

What is true of a man is equally true of a nation. The strength of a nation is its integrity, and no nation is stronger than the moral quality of the men who are its citizens. Always it comes back at last to the individual, who is a living stone in the wall of society and the state, making it strong or weak. By every act of injustice, by every lack of integrity, we weaken society and imperil the security and sanctity of the common life. By every noble act we make all sacred things more sacred and secure for ourselves and for those who come after us. The prophet Amos has a thrilling passage in which he lets us see how God tested the people which were of old by the Plumb-line; and by the same test we are tried:

"Thus He showed me: and, behold, the Lord stood upon a wall made by a plumb-line, with a plumb-line in His hand. And the Lord said unto me, 'Amos, what seest thou?' And I said, 'A plumb-line.' Then said the Lord, 'Behold, I will set a plumb-line in the midst of my people Israel: I will not again pass by them any more.'"

THE COMMON GAVEL

THE long Summer days are gone, Autumn is here, and the world takes up its task. The judge returns to his bench, the preacher to his pulpit, the man of affairs to his desk, the teacher to his school—the boys and girls following with no quick step. To some it is a joy, to others a grind, but all return to the work appointed them to do.

Last, but by no means least, the Lodge is opened, tiled and tested, and the sound of the Gavel in the East calls the Craft from refreshment to labor. Soon the noisy quarries will be busy, making ready the stone for a living Temple slowly rising without the sound of hammer or ax, built by the faith and labor of good and wise men as a shrine of fellowship and a shelter for the holy things of life.

As the Square is no doubt the oldest instrument of our science, so the Gavel it its oldest working tool—some trace it back to the rude ax of the stone age. How simple it is—just a piece of metal with a beating surface at one end and a cutting edge at the other, with a handle for better effect in use. Every Mason knows by heart the explanation of its meaning, given him in the First Degree:

The common Gavel is an instrument made use of by operative Masons, to break off the rough and

50

superfluous parts of stones, the better to fit them for the builder's use; but we, as Free and Accepted Masons, are taught to make use of it for the more noble and glorious purpose of divesting our minds and consciences of all the vices and superfluities of life, thereby fitting ourselves as living stones for that spiritual building, that house not made with hands, eternal in the heavens.

The words are simple; their meaning is plain—searching, too, when we think of the rough and superfluous things which need to be broken off and polished away from the best of us, before we are fit to be used by the Master of all good work. Alas, the words are so familiar that we too often forget how pointed and practical they are, teaching us the first necessity of the Craft—its need of clean and square men.

As we listened to those words for the first time, we did not realize how much meaning they held. No one can. There are so many delicate touches in Masonry, so many fine arts, that time is needed to see and appreciate them. Its business is to build men, taking the raw stuff of us and shaping it into forms of beauty and use. Before us it holds an ideal and plan of a Temple, into which it seeks to build our lives as stones. So it begins by using the Gavel, cutting away rough edges and breaking off ugly vices. Any man who knows himself at all knows how much it is needed, if he is to be a true man.

Nor did we notice, in the surprise of initiation, that the Gavel is also used by the Master of the Lodge. With it he opened and closed the Lodge;

with it he ruled. It is the symbol of his power. It is wonderful, if we think of it, how the humblest tool is put into the hand of the highest officer. So rough an instrument, the commonest in the quarry, hardly seems to typify a ruler. Yet in the three principal offices of the Lodge it is the symbol of authority. The Lodge is ruled not by a Square, still less by a Scepter, but by the sound of a common Gavel—only Masonry could have thought of a thing so beautiful.

Nor is it to be wondered at, because no tool in the kit of the Craft is used so often, and in so many ways, as the Gavel. Yet, as some one has observed, in all its variety of uses it remains the same. It is like a moral principle; it changes not. When the rough Ashlar is first taken from the quarry, the first tool applied to it, in the process of making it fit for its place, is the Gavel. Later, when the chisel must be used on the stone, the Gavel—or its big brother, the Maul—is employed to carry into effect the design of the worker. The Gavel is used in breaking large stones, or for chipping off tiny fragments; and it is equally effective for both ends.

While the Square, the Level, the Plumb has each one use and office, the Gavel is used in many ways, either by itself or with other tools, all the time. Cutting, chipping, driving, setting, it is always busy, always close to the hand of a Mason. Alike for suppression and for construction, its work never ends. It is the first tool of a craftsman, and the last he uses as Master of the Lodge, if he is counted worthy of that honor by the merit of his labor and the trust of his Brethren. The Gavel is capable of doing a great work, or of spoiling good material; it is at once the test and triumph of a Mason.

So, naturally, the Gavel is an emblem of power. It is an emblem of the power for good or ill in the hands of each man, being the commonest of tools; and also of the power of the Lodge in the hand of the Master. If wielded roughly, it means ruin. If wielded weakly, it means failure. If wielded wisely, and in the spirit of brotherly love, it is a wand of magic and a scepter of good will. Man is tempted and tested by power as by nothing else. Few are the men able to use it and not abuse it. No man is a Master Mason, or fit to be the Master of a Lodge, until he has learned to use the Gavel with dignity, self-control and gentle skill.

Since the Gavel is a symbol of the power both of Masons and of Masonry, it behooves us to ask how it is being used. Is the Gavel only an emblem and nothing more, like many another? Do we actually use it to cut away the vices and super-fluities of life which unfit us for the use and service of the Master Builder? Or, to put it otherwise, do we take our Masonry seriously, as a way of learning noble ways of thinking and living? Or is it a thing of rote, to be neglected when anything gets in its way—just another order to belong to? In short, is Masonry the power it should be in our lives and in the service of mankind?

As the Gavel sounds in the East, calling us to another year of Masonic labor, each of us ought to ask himself such questions as these, and answer them honestly in his own soul. What kind of a Lodge would my Lodge be if all its members were like me? What value would Masonry be to the world, if every one of its sons made the same use of it as we do? Do we answer the signs and summons sent us by the Lodge, as we vowed to do at its Altar? If not, what is a Masonic obligation worth, and what does it mean—nothing? Such questions tell us where we are in Masonry, and why we do so little with it.

Surely it is only fair to ourselves, as well as to the Craft, to ask ourselves such questions point blank. The Lodge opens on a new year, and we need to take stock betimes of our Masonic life and duty. What we lack more than anything else in America today, as citizens and as Masons, is a sense of personal responsibility for our laws and institutions, which enshrine the spirit and genius of our nation. If Masonry had a great place in the early days of the Republic, it was because Masons gave it a great place by serving the nation in its spirit. Truth wins if we are true to it and make it win.

Just now cynical writers in Europe are saying that American democracy must fail—that it cannot win. Of course it has not failed, else there would be more kings and more slaves in the world. But America is still on trial, and it will win only in so far as the village church, and the Lodge over the store, become real centers of brotherly love and neighborly co-operation and good will. When this sort of friendly and practical fellowship is abandoned by more than half of us, then our American democracy *will* fail and go to pieces, or else be only a shadow of itself.

Hear now some amazing facts which ought to

make us ponder. Less than half of our people ever attend, support, or are in any way associated with any kind of church—a fact to make a man stop and think, if he is aware of what happens to society when the influence of religion fails or grows dim. Not less amazing is the fact that hardly fifteen per cent of the Craft ever attend Lodge, or pay any heed to the sound of the Gavel in the East. It is appalling, such sheer neglect, by indifference and carelessness, of matters so vital to the well-being of the nation.

The remedy, so far as Masonry is concerned, is not far to seek. It lies not far away, but nearby, asking each of us to take a new vow in his own soul to make his Masonry more real, more active, more earnest both in his Lodge and in his life. Other way there is none, and it must begin with you and me. It is not Masonry that is at fault, but Masons who forget and fail of their duty. It is time for each of us to take up the Common Gavel, the first tool of a Mason, and divest our own soul of its apathy, ignorance, lack of zest and zeal.

What can we do to help the Master of our Lodge in the Masonic year now opening? At least we can go to Lodge and be a worker in the quarry; and our presence will increase, by so much, the influence of Masonry, and it will teach us to be helpers in the encouragement of brotherly love and fellowship. No man knows how far a simple act may go, gathering power as it goes. Our loyalty may be a tower of strength to fifty men who otherwise may lose heart and fall away. Our faithfulness will be an inspiration to the Master, who is human like ourselves, and pledged to bear many burdens on his heart. If each does his part, the sum of our labor will be very great, and the Craft will increase in usefulness and power among men.

At the end of the day, when the Lodge of our life is closed, and the sound of the Gavel is heard no more, the one thing no man will regret is that he lived in the fellowship of our gentle Craft, and labored in its service. Our life here amid sun and frost has meaning to ourselves, and worth to the Master of all Good Work, only as we invest such power as we have of light and leading to make the hard old world a little kinder for those who come after us.

> The New Age stands as yet
>   Half built against the sky,
> Open to every threat
>   Of storms that clamor by.
> Scaffolding veils the walls
>   And dim dust floats and falls
> As moving to and fro, their tasks
>   The Masons ply.

SECRECY

A N OLD Greek philosopher, when asked what he regarded as the most valuable quality to win and the most difficult to keep, replied, "To be secret and silent." If secrecy was difficult in the olden time, it is doubly difficult today, in the loud and noisy world in which we live, where privacy is almost unknown.

Secrecy is, indeed, a priceless but rare virtue, so little effort is made to teach and practice it. The world of today is a whispering gallery where everything is heard, a hall of mirrors where nothing is hid. If the ancients worshipped a god of silence, we seem about to set up an altar to the god of gossip.

Some one has said that if Masonry did no more than train its men to preserve sacredly the secrets of others confided to them as such—except where a higher duty demands disclosure—it would be doing a great work, and one which not only justifies its existence, but entitles it to the respect of mankind.

Anyway, no Mason needs to be told the value of secrecy. Without it, Masonry would cease to exist, or else become something so different from what it is as to be unrecognizable. For that reason, if no other, the very first lesson taught a candidate, and impressed upon him at every turn in unforgetable ways, is the duty of secrecy.

Yet, strictly speaking, Masonry is not a secret society, if by that we mean a society whose very existence is hidden. Everybody knows that the Masonic Fraternity exists, and no effort is made to hide the fact. Its organization is known; its temples stand in our cities; its members are proud to be known as Masons. Anyone may obtain from the records of Grand Lodge, if not from the printed reports of lodges, the names of the members of the Craft.

Nor can it be truly said that Masonry has any secret truth to teach, unknown to the best wisdom of the race. Most of the talk about esoteric Masonry misses the mark. When the story is told the only secret turns out to be some odd theory, some fanciful philosophy, of no real importance. The wisdom of Masonry is hidden, not because it is subtle, but because it is simple. Its secret is profound, not obscure.

As in mathematics there are primary figures, and in music fundamental notes, upon which everything rests, so Masonry is built upon the broad, deep, lofty truths upon which life itself stands. It lives, moves, and has its being in those truths. They are mysteries, indeed, as life and duty and death are mysteries; to know them is to be truly wise; and to teach them in their full import is the ideal at which Masonry aims.

Masonry, then, is not a secret society; it is a private order. In the quiet of the tiled lodge, shut away from the noise and clatter of the world, in an air of reverence and friendship, it teaches us the truths that make us men, upon which faith and character must rest if they are to endure the wind and weather of life. So rare is its utter simplicity that to many it is as much a secret as though it were hid behind a seven-fold veil, or buried in the depths of the earth.

What is secret in Masonry? The *method* of its teaching, the atmosphere it creates, the spirit it breathes into our hearts, and the tie it spins and weaves between man and man; in other words, the lodge and its ceremonies and obligations, its signs, tokens, and words—its power to evoke what is most secret and hidden in the hearts of men. No one can explain how this is done. We only know that it is done, and guard as a priceless treasure the method by which it is wrought.

It is the fashion of some to say that our ceremonies, signs and tokens are of little value; but that is not true. They are of profound importance, and we cannot too carefully protect them from profanation and abuse. The famous eulogy of the signs and tokens of Masonry by Benjamin Franklin was not idle eloquence. It is justified by the facts, and ought to be known and remembered:

"These signs and tokens are of no small value; they speak a universal language, and act as a passport to the attention and support of the initiated in all parts of the world. They cannot be lost so long as memory retains its power. Let the possessor of them be expatriated, ship-wrecked or imprisoned; let him be stripped of everything he has got in the world; still these credentials remain and are available for use as circumstances require.

"The great effects which they have produced are established by the most incontestable facts of history. They have stayed the uplifted hand of the destroyer; they have softened the asperities of the tyrant; they have mitigated the horrors of captivity; they have subdued the rancour of malevolence; and broken down the barriers of political animosity and sectarian alienation.

"On the field of battle, in the solitude of the uncultivated forests, or in the busy haunts of the crowded city, they have made men of the most hostile feelings, and most distant religions, and the most diversified conditions, rush to the aid of each other, and feel a social joy and satisfaction that they have been able to afford relief to a brother Mason."

What is equally true, and no less valuable, is that in the ordinary walks of everyday life they unite men and hold them together in a manner unique and holy. They open a door out of the loneliness in which every man lives. They form a tie uniting us to men of the Craft everywhere, and enable us to help one another, and others, in ways too many to name or count. They form a net-work of fellowship, friendship, and fraternity around the world. They add something lovely and fine to the life of each one of us, without which we should be poorer indeed.

Still, let us never forget that it is the spirit that gives life; the letter alone is empty. An old home means a thousand beautiful things to those who were brought up in it. Its very scenery and setting are sacred. The ground on which it stands is holy. But if a stranger buys it, these sacred things mean nothing to him. The spirit is gone, the glory has faded. Just so with the lodge. If it were opened to the curious gaze of the world, its beauty would be blighted, its power gone.

The secret of Masonry, like the secret of life, can be known only by those who seek it, serve it, live it. It cannot be uttered; it can only be felt and acted. It is, in fact, an open secret, and each man knows it according to his quest and capacity. Like all the things most worth knowing, no one can know it for another and no one can know it alone. It is known only in fellowship, by the touch of life upon life, spirit upon spirit, knee to knee, breast to breast, hand in hand.

For that reason, no one need be alarmed about any book written to expose Masonry. It is utterly harmless. The real secret of Masonry cannot be learned by prying eyes or curious inquiry. We do well to protect the privacy of the lodge; but the secret of Masonry can be known only by those who are ready and worthy to receive it. Only a pure heart and an honest mind can know it. Others seek it in vain, and never know it, though they be adepts in all the signs and tokens of every rite and rank of the Craft.

Indeed, so far from trying to hide its secret, Masonry is all the time trying to give it to the world, in the only way in which it can be given, through a certain quality of soul and character which it labors to create and build up. To the making of men, helping to self-discovery and self-development, all the offices of Masonry are dedicated. It is a quarry in which the rough stones of manhood are polished for use and beauty.

If Masonry uses the illusion of secrecy, it is because it knows that it is the nature of man to seek what is hidden and to desire what is forbidden. Even God hides from us, that in seeking Him amid the shadows of life we may find both Him and ourselves. The man who does not care enough for God to seek Him will never find Him, though He is not far from any one of us.

One who looks at Masonry in this way will find that his Masonic life is a great adventure. It is a perpetual discovery. There is something new at every turn, something new in himself as life deepens with the years; something new in Masonry as its meaning unfolds. The man who finds its degrees tedious and its ritual a rigmarole only betrays the measure of his own mind.

If a man knows God and man to the uttermost, even Masonry has nothing to teach him. As a fact the wisest man knows very little. The way is dim and no one can see very far. We are seekers after truth, and God has so made us that we cannot find the truth alone, but only in the love and service of our fellow men. Here is the real secret, and to learn it is to have the key to the meaning and joy of life.

Truth is not a gift; it is a trophy. To know it we must be true, to find it we must seek, to learn it we must be humble, and to keep it we must have a clear mind, a courageous heart, and the brotherly love to use it in the service of man.

FROM LEFT TO RIGHT

FOR some of us nothing in Masonry is more impressive than its very first rite, after an initiate has told in whom he puts his trust. It may be easily overlooked, but not to see it is to miss a part of that beauty we were sent to seek.

Surely he is a strange man who can witness it without deep feeling. The initiate is told that he can neither forsee nor prevent danger, but that he is in the hands of a true and trusty friend in whose fidelity he can with safety confide. It is literally true of the candidate, as it is of all of us.

As a mere ceremony it may mean nothing; as a symbol it means everything, if we regard initiation as we should, as a picture of man pursuing the journey of life, groping his dim and devious way out of the unreal into the real, out of darkness into light, out of the shadows of mortality into the way of life everlasting.

So groping, yet gently guided and guarded, man sets out on a mystic journey on an unseen road, traveling from the West to the East, and then from the East to the West by way of the South, seeking a City that hath foundations, where truth is known in fulness and life reveals both its meaning and its mystery. How profoundly true it is of the way we all must walk.

From the hour we are born till we are laid in the grave we grope our way in the dark, and none could find or keep the path without a guide. From how many ills, how many perils, how many pitfalls we are guarded in the midst of the years! With all our boasted wisdom and foresight, even when we fancy we are secure we may be in the presence of dire danger, if not of death itself.

Truly it does not lie in man to direct his path, and without a true and trusted Friend in whom we can confide, not one of us would find his way home. So Masonry teaches us, simply but unmistakably, at the first step as at the last, that we live and walk by Faith, not by sight; and to know that fact is the beginning of wisdom. Since this is so, since no man can find his way alone, in life as in the Lodge we must in humility trust our Guide, learn His ways, follow Him and fear no danger. Happy is the man who has learned that secret.

No wonder this simple rite is one of the oldest and most universal known among men. In all lands, in all ages, as far back as we have record, one may trace it, going back to the days when man thought the sun was God, or at least His visible outshining, whose daily journey through the sky, from the East to the West by way of the South, he followed in his faith and worship, seeking to win the favor of the Eternal by imitating his actions and reproducing His ways upon earth.

In Egypt, in India, in Greece, it was so. In the East, among the Magi, the priest walked three times around the altar, keeping it to his right, chanting hymns, as in the Lodge we recite words from the

Book of Holy Law. Some think the Druids had the same rite, which is why the stones at Stonehenge are arranged in circular form about a huge altar; and no doubt it is true.

What did man mean by the old and eloquent rite? All the early thought of man was mixed up with magic, and he is not yet free from it. One finds traces of it even in our own day. By magic is meant the idea that by imitating the ways of God we can actually control Him and make Him do what we want done. It is a false idea, but it still clings to much of our religion, as when men imagine that by saying so many prayers that they have gained so much merit.

Masonry is not magic; it is moral science. In the Lodge we are taught that we must learn the will of God, not in order to use Him for our ends, but the better to be used by Him for His ends. The difference may seem slight at first, but it is really the difference between a true and a false faith—between religion and superstition. Much of the religion of today is sheer superstition, in which magic takes the place of morals. In Masonry morality has first place, and no religion is valid without it.

As might be expected, a rite so old, so universal, so profoundly simple, has had many meanings read into it. The more the better; as a great teacher said of the Bible, the more meanings we find in it the richer we are. Some find in this old and simple rite a parable of the history of Masonry itself, which had its origin in the East and journeyed to the West, bringing the oldest wisdom of the world to bless and guide the newest lands.

Others see in it a symbol of the story of humanity, in its slow, fumbling march up out of savagery into the light of civilization; and it does lend itself to such a meaning. Often the race has seemed to be marching round and round, moving but making no progress; but that is only seeming. It does advance, in spite of the difficulties and obstructions in its path.

Still others think it is a parable of the life of each individual, showing our advance from youth with its rising sun in the East, which reaches its zenith in the meridian splendor of the South, and declines with the falling daylight to old age in the West. It is thus an allegory of the life of man upon the earth, its progress and its pathos, and true to fact.

All of these meanings are true and beautiful; but there is another and deeper meaning taught us more clearly in the old English rituals than in our own. It offers us an answer to the persistent questions: What am I? Whence came I? Whither go I? It tells us that the West is the symbol of this world; the East of the world above and beyond. Hence the colloquy in the First Degree:

"As a Mason, whence do you come?"

"From the West."

"Whither do you journey?"

"To the East."

"What is your inducement?"

"In quest of light."

That is, man supposes that his life originated in this world, and he answers accordingly. But that is because he is not properly instructed: he has not yet learned the great secret that the soul, our life-

star, had elsewhere its setting and comes from beyond this world of sense and time. It is only sent
into this dim world of sense and shadow for discipline and development—sent to find itself. So,
in the Third Degree, the answers are different, for
by that time the initiate has been taught a higher
truth:

"Whence do you come?"

"From the East."

"Whither are you wending?"

"To the West."

"What is your inducement?"

"To find that which is lost."

"Where do you hope to find it?"

"In the center."

Ah, here is real insight and understanding, to
know which is to have a key to much that we do
and endure in our life on earth; much which otherwise remains a riddle. Our life here in time and
flesh is a becoming, an awakening, an unfoldment,
a chance to find ourselves. It is, as Keats said, a
vale of soul-making, and the hard things that hit
and hurt us must be needed for our making, else
they would not be.

Nor do we walk with aimless feet, journeying nowhere, as the smart philosophers of our day tell us.
It is not a futile quest in which we are engaged.
And Masonry assures us that we are both guided
and guarded by a Friend who knows the way and
may be trusted to the end. Its promise is that the
veils will be removed from our eyes and the truth
made known to us, when we are ready and worthy
to receive it. But not until then.

It is a goodly teaching, tried by long ages and found to be wise and true. Alas, it is easily lost sight of and forgotten, and we need to learn it again and again. Here, too, Masonry is a wise teacher; it repeats, line upon line, precept upon precept. In every degree it shows us the march of the soul around the Altar, and then beyond it up the winding, spiral stair, and still beyond into the light and joy of the Eternal Life.

Save by the Old Road none attain the new,
From the Ancient Hills alone we catch the view.

"MORE LIGHT"

GOETHE was one of the myriad-minded men of our race, and a devout member of our gentle Craft. When he lay dying, as the soft shadow began to fall over his mind, he said to a friend watching by his bed: "Open the window and let in more light!" The last request of a great poet-Mason is the first quest of every Mason.

If one were asked to sum up the meaning of Masonry in one word, the only word equal to the task is—Light! From its first lesson to its last lecture, in every degree and every symbol, the mission of Masonry is to bring the light of God into the life of man. It has no other aim, knowing that when the light shines the truth will be revealed.

A Lodge of Masons is a House of Light. Symbolically it has no roof but the sky, open to all the light of nature and of grace. As the sun rises in the East to open and rule the day, so the Master rises in the East to open and guide the Lodge in its labor. All the work of the Lodge is done under the eye and in the name of God, obeying Him who made great lights, whose mercy endureth forever.

At the center of the Lodge, upon the Altar of Obligation, the Great Lights shine upon us, uniting the light of nature and the whiter light of revelation. Without them no Lodge is open in due form, and no business is valid. As the moon reflects the light of the sun, as the stars are seen only when the sun is hidden, so the Lesser Lights follow dimly where the Greater Lights lead.

To the door of the Lodge comes the seeker after light, hoodwinked and groping his way—asking to be led out of shadows into realities; out of darkness into light. All initiation is "bringing men to light," teaching them to see the moral order of the world in which they must learn their duty and find their true destiny. It is the most impressive drama on earth, a symbol of the divine education of man.

So through all its degrees, its slowly unfolding symbols, the ministry of Masonry is to make men "sons of light"—men of insight and understanding who know their way and can be of help to others who stumble in the dark. Ruskin was right: to see clearly is life, art, philosophy, and religion—all in one. When the light shines the way is plain, and the highest service to humanity is to lead men out of the confused life of the senses into the light of moral law and spiritual faith.

To that end Masonry opens upon its Altar the one great Book of Light, its pages aglow with "a light that never was on sea or land," shining through the tragedies of man and the tumults of time, showing us a path that shineth more and more unto the perfect day. From its first page to the last the key-word of the Bible is light, until, at the end, when the City of God is built, it has no need of the sun or the moon or the stars, for God is the light of it. Turning its pages we read:

And God said, Let there be Light; and there was light.

God is Light, and in Him is no darkness at all.

Thy word is a lamp unto my feet, and a light unto my path.

The entrance of Thy word giveth light.

The Lord is my light and my salvation; whom shall I fear.

There is light for the righteous, gladness for the true.

The Lord shall be to thee an everlasting light.

To them that sat in darkness, light is sprung up.

He stumbleth not, because he seeth the light.

I am come a light into the world.

While ye have the light believe in the light.

Let your light so shine before men.

To find the real origin of Masonry we must go far back into the past, back behind history. All the world over, at a certain stage of culture, men bowed down in worship of the sun, the moon, and the stars. In prehistoric graves the body was buried in a sitting posture, and always with the face toward the East, that the sleeper might be ready to spring up early to face the new and brighter day.

Such was the wonder of light and its power over man, and it is not strange that he rejoiced in its beauty, lifting up hands of praise. The Dawn was the first Altar in the old Light Religion of the race. Sunrise was an hour of prayer, and sunset, with its soft farewell fires, was the hour of sacrifice. After all, religion is a Divine Poetry, of which creeds are prose versions. Gleams of this old Light Religion shine all through Masonry, in its faith, in its sym-

bols, in the order and arrangement of a Lodge and
still more in its effort to organize the light of God
in the soul of man.

Such a faith is in accord with all the poetries
and pieties of the race. Light is the loveliest gift
of God to man; it is the mother of beauty and the
joy of the world. It tells man all that he knows,
and it is no wonder that his speech about it is
gladsome and grateful. Light is to mind what food
is to the body; it brings the morning, when the
shadows flee away, and the loveliness of the world
is unveiled.

Also, there is a mystery in light. It is not matter, but a form of motion; it is not spirit, though
it seems closely akin to it. Midway between the
material and the spiritual, it is the gateway where
matter and spirit pass and repass. Of all the glories
of nature it the most resembles God in its gentleness, its benignity, its pity, falling with impartial
benediction alike upon the just and the unjust, upon
the splendor of wealth and the squalor of poverty.

Yes, God is light, and the mission of Masonry
is to open the windows of the mind of man, letting
the dim spark within us meet and blend with the
light of God, in whom there is no darkness. There
is "a light that lighteth every man that cometh
into the world," as we learn in the Book of Holy
Law; but too often it is made dim by evil, error,
and ignorance, until it seems well nigh to have gone
out.

Hear now one of the most terrible words in the
Bible: "Eyes they have, but they do not see."
How many tragedies it explains, how many sor-

rows it accounts for. Most of our bigotries and brutalities are due to blindness. Most of the cruel wrongs we inflict upon each other are the blows and blunders of the sightless. Othello was blinded by jealousy, Macbeth by ambition, as we are apt to be blinded by passion, prejudice, or greed.

With merciful clarity Jesus saw that men do awful things without seeing what they do. "Father, forgive them, for they know not what they do." The pages of history are blacker than the hearts of the men that made history. Man is not as wicked as the wrongs he has done. Unless we see this fact, much of the history of man will read like the records of hell—remembering the atrocities of the Inquisition, the terrors of the French Revolution, and the red horror of Russia. It is all a hideous nightmare —man stumbling and striking in the dark.

No, humanity is more blind than bad. In his play, *St. Joan,* Shaw makes one of his characters say: "If you only saw what you think about, you would think quite differently about it. It would give you a great shock. I am not cruel by nature, but I did a very cruel thing once because I did not know what cruelty was like. I have been a different man ever since." Alas, he did not see what he had done until the hoodwink had been taken off.

More and more some of us divide men into two classes—those who see and those who do not see. The whole quality and meaning of life lies in what men see or fail to see. And what we see depends on what we are. In the Book of Holy Law the verb "to see" is close akin to the verb "to be," which is to teach us that character is the secret and source of insight. Virtue is vision; vice is blindness. "Blessed are the pure in heart, for they shall see God."

Thus our gentle Masonry, by seeking to "bring men to light," not simply symbolically but morally and spiritually, is trying to lift the shadow of evil, ignorance and injustice off the life of man. It is a benign labor, to which we may well give the best that we are or hope to be, toiling to spread the skirts of light that we and all men may see what is true and do what is right.

What the sad world needs—what each of us needs —is more light, more love, more clarity of mind and more charity of heart; and this is what Masonry is trying to give us. Once we take it to heart, it will help us to see God in the face of our fellows, to see the power of a lie and its inherent weakness because it is false, to see the glory of truth and its final victory: to see these things is to be a Mason, to see these things is to be saved.

> O Light that followeth all my way,
> I yield my flickering torch to Thee;
> My heart restores its borrowed ray,
> That in Thy sunshine's blaze its day
> May brighter, fairer be.

THE CABLE-TOW

THE word Cable-tow, we are told, is purely Masonic in its meaning and use. It is so defined in the dictionary, but not always accurately, which shows that we ought not to depend upon the ordinary dictionary for the truth about Masonic terms. Masonry has its own vocabulary and uses it in its own way. Nor can our words always be defined for the benefit of the profane.

Even in Masonic lore the word cable-tow varies in form and use. In an early pamphlet by Prichard, issued in 1730, and meant to be an exposure of Masonry, the cable-tow is called a "cable-rope"; and in another edition a "tow-line." The same word "tow-line" is used in a pamphlet called *A Defence of Masonry*, written, it is believed, by Anderson as a reply to Prichard about the same time. In neither pamphlet is the word used in exactly the form and sense in which it is used today; and in a note Prichard, wishing to make everything Masonic absurd, explains it as meaning "the roof of the mouth!"

In English lodges, the cable-tow, like the hoodwink, is used only in the first degree, and has no symbolical meaning at all, apparently. In our American lodges it is used in all three degrees, and has almost too many meanings. Some of our

American teachers—Pike among them—see no meaning in the cable-tow beyond its obvious use in leading an initiate into the Lodge, and the possible use of withdrawing him from it should he be unwilling or unworthy to advance.

To some of us this non-symbolical idea and use of the cable-tow is very strange, in view of what Masonry is in general, and particularly in its ceremonies of initiation. For Masonry is a chamber of imagery. The whole Lodge is a symbol. Every object, every act is symbolical. The whole fits together into a system of symbolism, by which Masonry veils, and yet reveals, the truth it seeks to teach to such as have eyes to see and are ready to receive it.

As far back as we can go in the history of initiation, we find the cable-tow, or something like it, used very much as it is used in a Masonic Lodge today. No matter what the origin and form of the word as we employ it may be—whether from the Hebrew "khabel," or the Dutch "cabel," both meaning a rope—the fact is the same. In India, in Egypt, in most of the Ancient Mysteries, a cord or cable was used in the same way and for the same purpose.

Its meaning, so far as we can make it out, seems to have been some kind of a pledge—a vow in which a man pledged his life. Even outside initiatory rites we find it so employed, as, for example, in a striking scene recorded in the Bible (1 Kings 20:31, 32), the description of which is almost Masonic. The king of Syria, Ben-hadad, had been defeated in battle by the king of Israel and his ser-

vants are making a plea for his life. They approach
the king of Israel "with ropes upon their heads,"
and speak of his "brother, Ben-hadad."

Why did they wear ropes, or nooses, on their
heads? Evidently to symbolize a pledge of some
sort, given in a Lodge or otherwise, between the
two kings, of which they wished to remind the king
of Israel. The king of Israel asked: "Is he yet
alive? he is my brother." Then we read that the
servants of the Syrian king watched to see if the
king of Israel made any sign, and, catching his sign,
they brought the captive king of Syria before him.
Not only was the life of the king of Syria spared,
but a new pledge was made between the two men.

The cable-tow, then, is the outward and visible
symbol of a vow in which a man has pledged his
life, or has pledged himself to save another life at
the risk of his own. Its length and strength are
measured by the ability of the man to fulfill his
obligation and his sense of the moral sanctity of
his obligation—a test, that is, both of his capacity
and of his character.

If a Lodge is a symbol of the world, and initiation
is our birth into the world of Masonry, the cable-
tow is not unlike the cord which unites a child to
its mother at birth; and so it is usually interpreted.
Just as the physical cord, when cut, is replaced by
a tie of love and obligation between mother and
child, so, in one of the most impressive moments
of initiation, the cable-tow is removed, because the
brother, by his oath at the Altar of Obligation, is
bound by a tie stronger than any physical cable.
What before was an outward physical restraint has

become an inward moral constraint. That is to say, force is replaced by love—outer authority by inner obligation—and that is the secret of security and the only basis of brotherhood.

The cable-tow is the sign of the pledge of the life of a man. As in his oath he agrees to forfeit his life if his vow is violated, so, positively, he pledges his life to the service of the Craft. He agrees to go to the aid of a Brother, using all the power in his behalf, "if within the length of his cable-tow," which means, if within the reach of his power. How strange that any one should fail to see symbolical meaning in the cable-tow! It is, indeed, the great symbol of the mystic tie which Masonry spins and weaves between men, making them Brothers and helpers one of another.

But, let us remember that a Cable-tow has two ends. If it binds a Mason to the Fraternity, by the same fact it binds the Fraternity to each man in it. The one obligation needs to be emphasized as much as the other. Happily, in our day we are beginning to see the other side of the obligation— that the Fraternity is under vows to its members to guide, instruct and train them for the effective service of the Craft and of humanity. Control, obedience, direction or guidance—these are the three meanings of the cable-tow, as it is interpreted by the best insight of the Craft.

Of course, by Control we do not mean that Masonry commands us in the sense that it uses force. Not at all. Masonry rules men as beauty rules an artist, as love rules a lover. It does not drive; it draws. It controls us, shapes us, through its human touch and its moral nobility. By the same method, by the same power it wins obedience and gives guidance and direction to our lives. At the Altar we take vows to follow and obey its high principles and ideals; and Masonic vows are not empty obligations—they are vows in which a man pledges his life and his sacred honor.

The old writers define the length of a cable-tow, which they sometimes call a "cable's length," variously. Some say it is seven hundred and twenty feet, or twice the measure of a circle. Others say that the length of the cable-tow is three miles. But such figures are merely symbolical, since in one man it may be three miles and in another it may as easily be three thousand miles—or to the end of the earth. For each Mason the cable-tow reaches as far as his moral principles go and his material conditions will allow. Of that distance each must be his own judge, and indeed each does pass judgment upon himself accordingly, by his own acts in aid of others.

Recently a man of science said that if the earth were held in its orbit by iron bars, they would have to be close together, not more than a foot apart, covering the entire surface. If, he said, these bars were twisted together into one gigantic cable, he doubted if it would be as strong as the invisible bond, or cable, by which the earth is held to its vast orbit. It was a striking way of teaching us that the cables that reach the longest and hold the strongest are invisible, and formed of forces with which men do not reckon, just because they are noiseless and unseen.

Just so, when the cable-tow of each Mason is joined with that of every other Mason, and all are united in one Cable of Kindness, it makes a bond of brotherhood the might of which no mortal can measure. It helps to hold the world together. It holds when other ties break, as it did in the Civil War in America. It is one of the holiest assets of humanity—a far-stretching Tie, mystical and unseen, yet more unbreakable than bands of steel, in which the obligation and loyalty and love of each of us is a strand.

> There is an unseen cord that binds
>   The whole wide world together;
> Through every human life it winds,
>   This one mysterious tether.
>
> There are no separate lives; the chain
>   Too subtle for our seeing,
> Unites us all upon the plane
>   Of universal being.

Such is the Divine cable-tow by which the world is held in its moral orbit. To discover that cord running through our own lives—your life and mine —uniting us with all the seekers after truth, all lovers of right, all servants of God and man, is the mission and blessing of Masonry. What is the length of our cable-tow? Who knows how far it reaches?

THE RITE OF DESTITUTION

NOTHING in Freemasonry is more beautiful in form or more eloquent in meaning than the First Degree. Its simplicity and dignity, its blend of solemnity and surprise, as well as its beauty of moral truth, mark it as a little masterpiece. Nowhere may one hope to find a nobler appeal to the native nobilities of a man. What we get out of Freemasonry, as of anything else, depends upon our capacity, and our response to its appeal; but it is hard to see how any man can receive the First Degree and pass out of the lodge room quite the same man as when he entered it.

What memories come back to us when we think of the time when we took our first step in Freemasonry. We had been led, perhaps, by the sly remarks of friends to expect some kind of horseplay, or the riding of a goat! but how different it was in reality. Instead of mere play-acting we discovered, by contrast, a ritual of religious faith and moral law, an allegory of life and a parable of those truths which lie at the foundations of manhood. Surely no man can ever forget the hour when, vaguely or clearly, the profound meaning of Freemasonry began slowly to unfold before his mind. Such an hour stands out as one of the vision-moments of life.

The whole meaning of initiation, of course, is an analogy of the birth, awakening and growth of the soul; its discovery of the purpose of life and the nature of the world in which it is to be lived. The lodge is the world as it was thought to be in the olden time, with its square surface and canopy of sky, its dark North and its radiant East; its center an Altar of obligation and prayer. The initiation, by the same token, is our advent from the darkness of prenatal gloom into the light of moral truth and spiritual faith, out of lonely isolation into a network of fellowships and relationships, out of a merely physical into a human and moral order. The cable-tow, by which we may be detained or removed should we be unworthy or unwilling to advance, is like the cord which joins a child to its mother at birth. Nor is it removed until, by the act of assuming the obligations and fellowships of the moral life, a new, unseen tie is spun and woven in the heart, uniting us, henceforth, by an invisible bond, to the service of our race in its moral effort to build a world of fraternal good will.

Such is the system of moral philosophy set forth in symbols to which the initiate is introduced, and in this light each emblem, each incident, should be interpreted. Thus Freemasonry gives a man at a time when it is most needed, if he be young, a noble, wise, time-tried scheme of thought and moral principle by which to read the meaning of the world and his duty in it. No man may hope to see it all at *once,* or once for all, and it is open to question whether any man lives long enough to think it through—for, like all simple things, it is deep and wonderful. In the actuality of the symbolism a man in the first degree of Freemasonry, as in the last, accepts the human situation, enters a new environment, with a new body of motive and experience. In short, he assumes his real vocation in the world and vows to live by the highest standard of values.

Like every other incident of initiation, it is in the light of the larger meanings of Freemasonry that we must interpret the Rite of Destitution. At a certain point in his progress every man is asked for a token of a certain kind, to be laid up in the archives of the lodge as a memorial of his initiation. If he is "duly and truly prepared" he finds himself unable to grant the request. Then, in one swift and searching moment, he realizes—perhaps for the first time in his life—what it means for a man to be actually destitute. For one impressive instant, in which many emotions mingle, he is made to feel the bewilderment, if not the humiliation, which besets one who is deprived of the physical necessities of life upon which, far more than we have been wont to admit, both the moral and social order depend. Then, by a surprise as sudden as before, and in a manner never to be forgotten, the lesson of the Golden Rule is taught—the duty of man to his fellow in dire need. It is not left to the imagination, since the initiate is actually put into the place of the man who asks his aid, making his duty more real and vivid.

At first sight it may seem to some that the lesson is marred by the limitations and qualifications which follow; but that is only seeming. Freemasons are under all the obligations of humanity, the most primary of which is to succor their fellow men in desperate plight. As Mohammed long ago said, the end of the world has come when man will not help man. But we are under special obligations to our brethren of the Craft, as much by the promptings of our hearts as by the vows we have taken. Such a principle, so far from being narrow and selfish, has the indorsement of the Apostle Paul in his exhortations to the early Christian community. In the Epistle to the Galatians we read: "As we have therefore opportunity, let us do good unto all men, especially unto them who are of the household of faith." It is only another way of saying that "charity begins at home," and for Masons the home is the lodge.

So, then, the destitute to which this Rite refers, and whose distress the initiate is under vows to relieve, as his ability may permit, are a definite and specific class. They are not to be confused with those who are poverty-stricken by reason of criminal tendencies or inherent laziness. That is another problem, in the solution of which Masons will have their share and do their part—a very dark problem, too, which asks for both patience and wisdom. No, the needy which this Rite requires that we aid are "all poor, distressed, worthy Masons, their widows and orphans"; that is, those who are destitute through no fault of their own, but as the result of untoward circumstance. They are those who, through accident, disease or disaster, have become unable, however willing and eager, to meet their obligations. Such are deserving of

charity in its true Masonic sense, not only in the
form of financial relief, but also in the form of
companionship, sympathy and love. If we are bid-
den to be on our guard against impostors, who
would use Masonry for their own ends, where there
is real need our duty is limited only by our ability
to help, without injury to those nearest to us.

A church, if it be worthy of the name, opens its
doors to all kinds and conditions of folk, rich and
poor alike, the learned and the unlearned. But a
lodge of Masons is different, alike in purpose and
function. It is made up of picked men, selected
from among many, and united for unique ends. No
man ought to be allowed to enter the Order unless
he is equal to its demands, financially as well as
mentally and morally, able to pay its fees and dues,
and to do his part in its work of relief. Yet no set
of men, however intelligent and strong, are exempt
from the vicissitudes and tragedies of life. Take, for
example, Anthony Sayer, the first Grand Master of
the Grand Lodge of England. Towards the end of
his life he met with such reverses that he became
tiler of Old King's Arms Lodge, No. 28, and it is
recorded that he was assisted "out of the box of
this Society." Such a misfortune, or something
worse, may overtake any one of us, without warning
or resource.

Disasters of the most appalling kind befall men
every day, leaving them broken and helpless. How
often have we seen a noble and able man suddenly
smitten down in mid life, stripped not only of his
savings but of his power to earn, as the result of
some blow no mortal wit could avert. There he

lies, shunted out of active life when most needed
and most able and willing to serve. Life may any
day turn Ruffian and strike one of us such a blow,
disaster following fast and following faster, until
we are at its mercy. It is to such experiences that
the Rite of Destitution has reference, pledging us
to aid as individuals and as lodges; and we have
a right to be proud that our Craft does not fail in
the doing of good. It is rich in benevolence, and
it knows how to hide its labors under the cover of
secrecy, using its privacy to shield itself and those
whom it aids.

Yet we are very apt, especially in large lodges,
or in the crowded solitude of great cities, to lose
the personal touch, and let our charity fall to the
level of a cold, distant almsgiving. When this is
so charity becomes a mere perfunctory obligation,
and a lodge has been known to vote ten dollars for
the relief of others and fifty dollars for its own
entertainment! There is a Russian story in which
a poor man asked aid of another as poor as himself:
"Brother, I have no money to give you, but let
me give you my hand," was the reply. "Yes, give
me your hand, for that, also, is a gift more needed
than all others," said the first; and the two forlorn
men clasped hands in a common need and pathos.
There was more real charity in that scene than in
many a munificent donation made from a sense of
duty or pride.

Indeed, we have so long linked charity with the
giving of money that the word has well night lost
its real meaning. In his sublime hymn in praise
of charity, in the thirteenth chapter of First Corin-

thians, St. Paul does not mention money at all,
except to say "and though I bestow all my goods
to feed the poor, and have not charity, it profiteth
me nothing." Which implies that a man may give
all the money he possesses and yet fail of that
Divine grace of Charity. Money has its place and
value, but it is not everything, much less the sum
of our duty, and there are many things it cannot
do. A great editor sent the following greeting at
the New Year:

"Here is hoping that in the New Year there will
be nothing the matter with you that money cannot
cure. For the rest, the law and the prophets con-
tain no word of better rule for the health of the
soul than the adjuration: Hope thou a little, fear
not at all, and love as much as you can."

Surely it was a good and wise wish, if we think
of it, because the things which money cannot cure
are the ills of the spirit, the sickness of the heart,
and the dreary, dull pain of waiting for those who
return no more. There are hungers which gold
cannot satisfy, and blinding bereavements from
which it offers no shelter. There are times when
a hand laid upon the shoulder, "in a friendly sort
of way," is worth more than all the money on earth.
Many a young man fails, or makes a bad mistake,
for lack of a brotherly hand which might have held
him up, or guided him into a wiser way.

The Rite of Destitution! Yes, indeed; but a man
may have all the money he needs, and yet be destitute of faith, of hope, of courage; and it is our
duty to share our faith and courage with him. To
fulfill the obligations of this Rite we must give not

simply our money, but ourselves, as Lowell taught in "The Vision of Sir Launfal," writing in the name of a Great Brother who, though he had neither home nor money, did more good to humanity than all of us put together—and who still haunts us like the dream of a Man we want to be.

"The Holy Supper is kept indeed,
In whatso we share with another's need;
Not that which we give, but what we share,
For the gift without the giver is bare;
Who bestows himself with his alms feeds three:
Himself, his hungering neighbor, and Me!"

THE NORTH EAST CORNER

SURELY no Mason ever forgets the moment
when he is placed in the North East Corner of
the Lodge, and hears the Master say that he there
stands a just and upright Mason. It is one of the
thrills along the great journey of initiation, a point
at which the idea and purpose of Masonry begin to
take shape in the mind.

A thrill of joy is felt in the Lodge, not only by
the initiate but by the Master and the Brethren,
as if a son had been born, or a new friend found;
as when a pilgrim pauses to rejoice in so much of a
journey done. And naturally so, because the Corner
Stone of a Masonic life has been laid.

Always, as far back as we can go in the story of
mankind, the laying of a Corner Stone has been a
happy event. It has always been celebrated with
solemn and joyous rites. It is the basis of a new
building, the beginning of a new enterprise; and the
good will of God is invoked to bless the builders and
the building.

How much more, then, should it be so when a
man takes the first step out of Darkness toward the
Light, and begins the adventure of a new life!
More important by far than temple or cathedral is
the building of a moral character and a spiritual
personality. Stones will rot and temples crumble

under the attrition of time, but moral qualities and spiritual values belong to the Eternal Life.

The initiate stands in the North East Corner on a foundation of Justice, the one virtue by which alone a man can live with himself or with his fellows. Without it no structure will stand, in architecture, as Ruskin taught us, much less in morals. In the Rite of Destitution he has learned to love Mercy, and at the Altar of Obligation prayer has been offered, in fulfillment of the words of the prophet:

"He hath shewed thee, O man, what is good; and what doth the Lord require of thee, but to do justly, and to love mercy, and to walk humbly with thy God?"

In the North East Corner the initiate stands midway between the North, the place of Darkness, and the East, the place of Light, whence healing, revealing rays fall upon the life of man. Such is his position, symbolically, and rightly so. He is an Entered Apprentice, a beginner in the Masonic art, neither in the Dark nor in the Light. He has come out of the Darkness, his face set toward the Light, and his quest is for more Light, with yet much light to dawn upon him.

What is life for? To live, of course; and only by living it do we learn what it is for, much less how to live it. It is ever an adventure, a new adventure for each man, despite the millions that have lived before us, since, as Keats said about poets, "we never really understand fine things until we have gone the same steps as the author." Only by living can we learn what life is, verifying the wisdom of ages alike by our virtues and our vices.

Yet it means much to have the wisdom learned by ages of living taught us in symbols and told us in a story, as it is taught us and told us in a Masonic lodge. It brings to us the truth tried by time and tragedy, and the principles wrought out and discovered by the race in its long experience. It gives us a plan, a picture, a prophecy, and the fellowship of men going the same road.

The initiate stands Erect in the North East Corner, upright and ready to receive his working tools, a son of the Light, himself a living stone to be polished. What is more wonderful, what more beautiful, than Youth standing erect before God—not cringing, not groveling—seeking the Light by which to make its way through the dim country of this world to the city that hath foundations! Truly, our Masonry is the organized poetry of faith!

But why the North East Corner? Would not some other corner of the lodge do as well? Perhaps it would, but Masonry is very old, going back into a time far gone, when ordinary things had meanings, real or imaginary, beyond their practical use. Such a question opens a window into things quaint, curious, and even awful, and all sorts of explanations are offered us, some of which may be named.

For example, Albert Pike spread out the map of the old world of the East—the mystical territory whence so many of our symbols and legends have come—and found that "the Apprentice represents the Aryan race in its original home on the highlands of Pamir, in the north of that Asia termed

Orient, at the angle whence, upon two great lines of emigration South and West, they flowed forth in successive waves to conquer and colonize the world."

Well, what of it, interesting though it may be as a fact of long ago, if a fact it is? What truth can it teach us to our profit, beyond the suggestion that the House of Initiation took the form of the world as it was then mapped in the mind, and that the procession of initiation follows the line of march of a conquering race? It may be valuable, as preserving the dim outline of ancient history—but not otherwise.

Another student, seeking the secret of Masonry in solar symbolism and mythology, looks at the same map of the eastern world, in the frame of an Oblong Square, studying the movements of the Sun from season to season. He finds that the point farthest North and the point farthest South on the map mark the Summer and Winter Solstices, respectively. In other words, the North East Corner of the world, as then mapped, is the point in the annual course of the Sun when it reaches the extreme northern limit; the longest day in the year, which in Masonry we dedicate to St. John the Baptist, the prophet of righteousness.

Then, turning to the history of religion, he finds, not unnaturally, many rites of primitive peoples— magical rituals and Midsummer Night Dreams— celebrating the Summer Solstice. Many hints and relics of the old Light Religion are preserved for us in Masonry—rays of its faiths and fictions—one of them being that of the North East Corner of the

Universe, and so of the Lodge of which it is a symbol, is the seat of the Sun-God in the prime of his power.

So, too, the North East Corner, as the throne of God in the hour of his majesty, became a place unique in the symbols of man, having special virtue and sanctity. As we read in the Institutes of Menu: "If he has any incurable disease, let him advance in a straight path towards the invincible northeast point, feeding on water and air till his mortal frame totally decay, and his soul become united with the Supreme." What more appropriate place from which to start an edifice, or to place an Apprentice as he begins to build the temple of his Masonic life?

Also, because of such magical ideas associated with the North East Corner, it was a cruel custom for ages to bury a living human being under the corner stone of a building, to mollify the gods, and, later, as a token of the sacrifice involved in all building. Horrible as the custom was, here no doubt was a crude sense of the law of sacrifice running through all human life, never to be escaped, even by the loftiest souls, as we see on a dark cross outside the city gate.

In crude ages all things were crude; even the holiest insights took awful shapes of human sacrifice. Life is costly, and man has paid a heavy price for the highest truth. For there is a law of heavenly death by which man advances—the death, that is, of all that is unheavenly within him—that the purer, clearer truth may rise. Evermore, by a law of dying into life, man grows—dying to his lower, lesser self and releasing the angel hidden within him.

Thinking of all these strands of thought and faith and sorrow woven into the symbolism of the lodge, how can any one watch without emotion as the Apprentice takes his place, upright and eager, in the North East Corner. There he stands, against a background of myth and symbol and old sacrifice, erect before God, and one thinks of the great words in the book of Ezekiel:

"And God said unto me, Son of Man, stand upon thy feet, and I will speak unto thee. And the spirit entered into me when he spake unto me, and set me upon my feet, that I heard him that spake unto me."

Such is the challenge of God to the manhood of man, asking him to stand erect and unafraid, and commune as friend with friend. Alas, it is not easy to keep the upright posture, physically or morally, in the midst of the years with their blows and burdens. At last, a dark Ruffian lays us low in death, and only the Hand of God, with its strong grip, can lift us from a dead level and set us on our feet forever. So, at least, Masonry teaches us to believe and live:

Lord, I believe
Man is no little thing
That, like a bird in spring,
Comes fluttering to the Light of Life,
And out of the darkness of long death.
The Breath of God is in him,
And his agelong strife
With evil has a meaning and an end.
Though twilight dim his vision be

Yet can he see Thy Truth,
And in the cool of evening, Thou, his friend,
Dost walk with him, and talk
(Did not the Word take flesh?)
Of the great destiny
That waits him and his race.
In days that are to be
By grace he can achieve great things,
And, on the wings of strong desire,
Mount upward ever, higher and higher,
Until above the clouds of earth he stands,
And stares God in the face.

THE MASTER'S PIECE

IN the olden time it was no easy matter for a man to become a Freemason. He had to win the right by hard work, technical skill, and personal worth. Then, as now, he had to prove himself a freeman of lawful age and legitimate birth, of sound body and good repute, to be eligible at all. Also, he had to bind himself to serve under rigid rules for seven years, his service being at once a test of his character and a training for his work. If he proved incompetent or unworthy, he was sent away.

In all operative lodges of the Middle Ages, as in the guilds of skilled artisans of the same period, young men entered as Apprentices, vowing absolute obedience, for the lodge was a school of the seven sciences, as well as of the art of building. At first the Apprentice was little more than a servant, doing the most menial work, and if he proved himself trustworthy and proficient his wages were increased; but the rules were never relaxed, "except at Christmastime," as the Old Charges tell us, when there was a period of freedom duly celebrated with feast and frolic.

The rules by which an Apprentice pledged himself to live, as we find them recorded in the Old Charges, were very strict. He had first to confess his faith in God, vowing to honor the Church, the State and the Master under whom he served, agreeing not to absent himself from the service of the Order save with the license of the Master. He must be honest and upright, faithful in keeping the secrets of the Craft and the confidence of his fellows. He must not only be chaste, but must not marry or contract himself to any woman during the term of his apprenticeship. He must be obedient to the Master without argument or murmuring, respectful to all Freemasons, avoiding uncivil speech, free from slander and dispute. He must not frequent any tavern or alehouse, except it be upon an errand of the Master, or with his consent.

Such was the severe rule under which an Apprentice learned the art and secrets of the Craft. After seven years of study and discipline, either in the lodge or at the Annual Assembly (where awards were usually made), he presented his "Masterpiece," some bit of stone or metal carefully carved, for the inspection of the Master, saying, "Behold my experience!" By which he meant the sum of his experiments. He had spoiled many a bit of stone. He had dulled the edge of many a tool. He had spent laborious nights and days, and the whole was in that tiny bit of work. His masterpiece was carefully examined by the Masters assembled and if it was approved he was made a Master Mason, entitled to take his kit of tools and go out as a workman, a Master and Fellow of his Craft. Not, however, until he had selected a Mark by which his work could be identified, and renewed his vows to the Order in which he was now a Fellow.

The old order was first Apprentice, then Master, then Fellow—mastership being, in the early time, not a degree conferred, but a reward of skill as a workman and of merit as a man. The reversal of the order today is due, no doubt, to the custom of the German Guilds, where a Fellow Craft was required to serve two additional years as a journeyman before becoming a Master. No such custom was known in England. Indeed, the reverse was true, and it was the Apprentice who prepared his masterpiece, and if it was accepted, he became a Master. Having won his mastership, he was entitled to become a Fellow—that is, a peer and Fellow of the Craft which hitherto he had only served. Hence, all through the Old Charges, the order is "Masters and Fellows," but there are signs to show that a distinction was made according to ability and skill.

For example, in the Matthew Cooke MS. we read that it had been "ordained that they who were passing of cunning should be passing honored," and those less skilled were commanded to call the more skilled "Masters." Then it is added, "They that were less of wit should not be called servant nor subject, but Fellow, for nobility of their gentle blood." After this manner our ancient brethren faced the fact of human inequality of ability and initiative. Those who were of greater skill held a higher position and were called Masters, while the masses of the Craft were called Fellows. A further distinction must be made between a "Master" and a "Master of the Work," now represented by the Master of the lodge. Between a Master and the

Master of the Work there was no difference, of course, except an accidental one; they were both Masters and Fellows. Any Master could become a Master of the Work provided he was of sufficient skill and had the fortune to be chosen as such either by the employer or the lodge, or both.

What rite or ritual, if any, accompanied the making of a Master in the old operative lodges is still a matter of discussion. In an age devoted to ceremonial it is hard to imagine such an important event without its appropriate ceremony, but the details are obscure. But this is plain enough: all the materials out of which the degrees were later developed existed, if not in drama, at least in legend. Elaborate drama would not be necessary in an operative lodge. Even today, much of what is acted out in an American lodge, is merely recited in an English lodge. Students seem pretty well agreed that from a very early time there were two ceremonies, or degrees, although, no doubt, in a much less elaborate form than now practiced. As the Order, after the close of the cathedral-building program, passed into its speculative character, there would naturally be many changes and much that was routine in an operative lodge became ritual in a speculative lodge.

This is not the time to discuss the origin and development of the Third Degree, except to say that those who imagine that it was an invention fabricated by Anderson and others at the time of the revival of Masonry, in 1717, are clearly wrong. Such a degree could have been invented by anyone familiar with the ancient Mystery Religions; but it could never have been imposed upon the Craft, unless it harmonized with some previous ceremony, or, at least, with ideas, traditions and legends familiar and common to the members of the Craft. That such ideas and traditions did exist in the Craft we have ample evidence. Long before 1717 we hear hints of "The Master's Part," and those hints increase as the office of Master of the Work lost its practical aspect after the cathedral-building period. What was the Master's Part? Unfortunately we cannot discuss it in print; but nothing is plainer than that we do not have to go outside of Masonry itself to find the materials out of which all three degrees, as they now exist, were developed.

Masonry was not invented; it grew. Today it unfolds its wise and good and beautiful truth in three noble and impressive degrees, and no man can take them to heart and not be ennobled and enriched by their dignity and beauty. The first lays emphasis upon that fundamental righteousness without which a man is not a man, but a medley of warring passions—that purification of heart which is the basis alike of life and religion. The Second lays stress upon the culture of the mind, the training of its faculties in the quest of knowledge, without which man remains a child. The Third seeks to initiate us, symbolically, into the eternal life, making us victors over death before it arrives. The First is the Degree of Youth, the Second the Degree of Manhood, the Third the consolation and conquest of Old Age, when the evening shadows fall and the Eternal World and its unknown adventure draw near.

What, then, for each of us today, is meant by
the Master's Piece? Is it simply a quaint custom
handed down from our ancient brethren, in which
we learn how an Apprentice was made a Master
of his Craft? It is that indeed, but much more.
Unless we have eyes to see a double meaning everywhere in Masonry, a moral application and a spiritual suggestion, we see little or nothing. But if we
have eyes to see it is always a parable, an allegory,
a symbol, and the Master's Piece of olden-time becomes an emblem of that upon which every man
is working all the time and everywhere, whether he
is aware of it or not—his character, his personality,
by which he will be tested and tried at last. Character, as the word means, is something carved,
something wrought out of the raw stuff and hard
material of life. All we do, all we think, goes into
the making of it. Every passion, every aspiration
has to do with it. If we are selfish, it is ugly. If
we are hateful, it is hideous. William James went
so far as to say that just as the stubs remain in
the check book, to register the transaction when
the check is removed, so every mental act, every
deed becomes a part of our being and character.
Such a fact makes a man ponder and consider what
he is making out of his life, and what it will look
like at the end.

Like the Masons of old, apprenticed in the school
of life, we work for "a penny a day." We never
receive a large sum all at once, but the little reward
of daily duties. The scholar, the man of science,
attains truth, not in a day, but slowly, little by
little, fact by fact. In the same way, day by day,

act by act, we make our character, by which we shall stand judged before the Master of All Good Work. Often enough men make such a bad botch of it that they have to begin all over again. The greatest truth taught by religion is the forgiveness of God, which erases the past and gives another chance. All of us have spoiled enough material, dulled enough enough tools and made enough mistakes to teach us that life without charity is cruel and bitter.

Goethe, a great Mason, said that talent may develop in solitude, but character is created in society. It is the fruit of fellowship. Genius may shine aloof and alone, like a star, but goodness is social, and it takes two men and God to make a brother. In the Holy Book which lies open on our altar we read: "No man liveth unto himself; no man dieth unto himself." We are tied together, seeking that truth which none may learn for another, and none may learn alone. If evil men can drag us down, good men can lift us up. No one of us is strong enough not to need the companionship of good men and the consecration of great ideals. Here lies, perhaps, the deepest meaning and value of Masonry; it is a fellowship of men seeking goodness, and to yield ourselves to its influence, to be drawn into its spirit and quest, is to be made better than ourselves.

Amid such influences each of us is making his Master's Piece. God is all the time refining, polishing, with strokes now tender, now terrible. That is the meaning of pain, sorrow, death. It is the chisel of the Master cutting the rough stone. How hard the mallet strikes, but the stone becomes a pillar, an arch, perhaps an altar emblem. "Him that overcometh, I will make a pillar in the temple of my God." The masterpiece of life, at once the best service to man and the fairest offering to God, is a pure, faithful, heroic, beautiful Character.

THE CRADLE AND THE LODGE

ONCE again the march of days has brought us near to the day of all the year the best—Christmas Day, with its gentleness, its joy, and its good will. We have national holidays of deep historic meaning and beauty; but Christmas is a day in the calendar of humanity—a day dedicated to childhood and the home.

Only one other day can compete with Christmas in our regard, and that is Easter Day, with its "song of those who answer not, however we may call"; and being days of Faith, they are both days of hope and forward-looking thoughts. If Easter teaches us hope in the life to come, Christmas asks us to hope for the life that now is. How fitting it is that we have a festival of the dawn of life linked in our faith with the Easter hope at sunset.

The hope of the world is the child. Here the everlasting enterprise of education finds its reason and sanction. The child holds in his chubby hand the future of the race, our hope of social beauty and human welfare. He is the custodian of whatever of truth and worth we may bequeath to the times to come; the window in which, at sunset, we see the morning light of a new day. In him we

live again, if in no other way—save in the memory
of God, who does not forget. He is our earthly
immortality.

No man does more to bring the kingdom of
heaven to earth than he who takes care that his
child is born in purity and honor. A child nobly
and sweetly born will not need to be born again,
unless some killing sin slay him by the way. No
wonder the greatest religion in the world makes
a Cradle its shrine, and finds in the heart of a little
child its revelation of God and its hope for man.

What unaccountable blessings came to the world
with the birth of one little Child, born of poor par-
ents in an obscure nook in a small country long
ago, and who, without sword or pen, divided the
history of man into before and after. What a
strange power of influence lay sleeping in that
Manger-Cradle, to be set free in a short life, which
has changed the moral and spiritual climate of the
earth. There shone a light that can never fail, revealing the Spirit of God and the meaning of life,
making mother and child forever sacred, and softening the hard heart of the world. It is a scene
to sanctify the world, so heavenly yet so homey,
and it has done more than any other one influence
to purify the life of man.

No man of us—whatever his religion—but is
touched to tenderness by that picture of a Child,
a Mother hovering near, a Father in the background,
and a Star standing sentinel in the sky. Before
that day the order was Father, Mother, Child—
now it is Child, Mother, Father. Such power one
Child had to alter the old order of the world. They

are indeed wise men who follow such a starry truth
and bow at such a shrine, linking a far-off wandering star with the Cradle of a little Child.

For Christmas is both a fact and a symbol. It
is the greatest fact of history and the symbol of
the deepest truth man can know on earth. It tells
of a time when the idea of God was born anew
in the mind of man. Think how you will about
the Babe in the Manger, debate as you like about
the facts of his life, it is a fact that since Jesus
lived God has been nearer to the life of man, more
real and more lovable. The Christmas scene shows
us that God is not off up in the sky, but near by,
even in our hearts if we are wise enough to make
room for Him.

If we open the Book of Holy Law we learn in
the Old Testament that man lives in God, who is
the home of the soul from generation to generation.
It is a profound truth. It makes the world home-
like. It unites us as a family under the shelter of
a Divine Love. In the New Testament we learn
that God lives in man, and that is the greatest
discovery man has ever made. For unless there is
something of God in man—in every man—we can
not find God, much less know Him. The revelation
of God in humanity is the basis of all democracy
worthy of the name, and the only hope of brotherhood among men.

No wonder Christmas is a day of music and joy.
It brings heaven and earth together, and teaches
us that no hope of the human heart is too high, no
faith too holy, to be fulfilled by the love that moves
the sun and the stars. God in man—here is the

secret of all our hope for the better day to be when man will no longer make war, but will live in fraternity and good will.   Unless the Divine dwells in man, there is no strand strong enough to hold against the dark forces which fight against peace. God in man—here is the mystic tie by which man is bound to man in bonds of mutual need and service and hope.

So we begin to see what the Cradle has to do with the Lodge.   Indeed, as all the wise teachers of the Craft agree, the Lodge is a Cradle and initiation is birth, by which man makes his advent into a new world.   The cable-tow, by which we may be detained or removed should we be unworthy or unwilling to advance, is like the cord which joins a child to its mother at birth.   Nor is it removed until, by a voluntary act, we assume the obligations of a man, and a new unseen tie is woven in our hearts.   Henceforth we are united by an invisible bond, lighter than air but stronger than steel, to the service of the craft and the race.

In the First Degree we are symbolically born out of darkness into the light of moral truth and duty, out of a merely physical into a spiritual world. Symbolically we enter into a new environment, as the child does at birth, with a new body of motive and law, taking vows to live by the highest standard of values.   In other words, an Entered Apprentice discovers his own Divinity—learns who he is, why he is here, and what he is here to do.   No secret that science can uncover is half so thrilling.   Finding a new star out on the edge of the sky is nothing alongside the discovery of God in the soul.

In the same way, in the Third Degree, we are symbolically initiated into the eternal life in time. Actually we pass through death and beyond it while yet walking upon the earth! God is here within us, eternity is now, and death is only the shadow of life—such is the secret of Masonry. Once a man really discovers it, and governs himself accordingly, he is a free man—erect, unafraid, happy. Thus Masonry, in its own way, teaches the truth of Christmas and Easter Day, and deeper truth it is not given us to know or imagine. It lights up the world with joy, and changes even dull death into a last enchantment.

God in man, the soul of man a Cradle of the Eternal Love—what higher truth has man ever dreamed! By the same token, the hope of the world, and of each of us, lies in the birth and growth of the Divine in man—in your life and mine—refining lust into love, and greed into goodness. Also, since we have the same spark of Divinity within us, and the same starry ideals above us—even as we are made of the same dust, and know the same dogs of passion at our heels—it behooves us to love one another, to seek to know, to understand, and to help our fellow man. For here, in truth, is the basis and prophecy of brotherhood.

God be thanked for a Truth so Divine that it lends dignity to our fleeting days—for a day of poetry in the midst of gray days of prose. On that day we work and plan that the child may have his toy, and the friend his token of our love; and, forgetting ourselves, we learn that our life on other days is but a muddled memory of what it ought to be. One day, at least, we seek out the poor, the sick, the weary and world-broken, and find in service a joy we know not in selfishness.

Blessed Christmas Day—symbol of the Eternal Child and "the Cradle endlessly rocking." It takes us down from our towering pride and teaches us humility and sweet charity. It brings us to a simplicity of faith in which we find peace. It rebukes our bitter wisdom because it is unholy and unhopeful. It brings across the years a memory of days when life was stainless, and gives us hope that some time, somewhere, we shall find again the secret we have lost.

O great heart of God,
　　Once vague and lost to me,
Why do you throb with my throb tonight,
　　Is this land Eternity?

O little heart of God,
　　Sweet intruding stranger,
You are laughing in my human breast,
　　A Christ-Child in a manger.

Heart, dear heart of God,
　　Beside you now I kneel,
Strong heart of faith, O heart of mine,
　　Where God has set His seal.

Wild, thundering heart of God,
　　Out of my doubt I come,
And my foolish feet with the prophet's feet
　　March with the prophet's drum.

AN ERRING BROTHER

NEXT to the word Mother, no word in our language has more meaning and music in it than the word Brother. It is from above, and it reaches to the deep places of the heart. It is religion, on its human side; and in it lies the hope of humanity. The highest dream of the prophets is of a time when men shall be Brothers.

When used Masonically, the word Brother has a depth and tenderness all its own, unique and beautiful beyond words. It tells of a tie, mystical but mighty, which Masonry spins and weaves between man and man, which no one can define and few can resist. In time of joy it is a bond of happiness; in time of sorrow it is a tether of sympathy and a link of loyalty.

Of course, like all other words, it is common enough, and may be glibly used without regard to its real meaning. Like the word God, it may be a coin worn smooth, or a flower faded. But when its meaning is actually and fully felt, no other word is needed among us, except on occasions of high Masonic ceremony, when we add the word Worshipful, or some other term of title or rank.

No other word has a finer import or a more ample echo, expressive of the highest relationship, in which dignity and devotion unite. If we are really

Brothers, all the rest may go by the board, save for sake of ceremony. If we are not truly Brothers, all titles are empty and of no avail. For that reason, to omit the word Brother, when speaking Masonically, is not only a lack of courtesy, but shows a want of fineness of feeling.

What does the word Brother mean, Masonically? It means the adoption of a man into an inner circle of friendship, by a moral and spiritual tie as close and binding as the tie of common birth and blood between two brothers in a family. Nothing else, nothing less; and this implies a different attitude the one to the other—related not distant, united not opposed, natural and unrestrained—wherein are revealed what the old writers used to call "the happy and beneficial effects of our Ancient and Honorable Institution."

Since this is so, surely we ought to exercise as much caution and judgment in bringing a new member into the Lodge, as we do in inviting an outsider into the family circle. Carelessness here is the cause of most of our Masonic ills, frictions, and griefs. Unless we are assured beyond all reasonable doubt that a man is a brotherly man to whom Masonry will appeal, and who will justify our choice, we ought not to propose his name or admit him to our fellowship.

Still, no man is perfect; and the Lodge is a moral workshop in which the rough Ashlar is to be polished for use and beauty. If the Lodge had been too exacting, none of us would have gained admission. At best we must live together in the Lodge, as elsewhere, by Faith, Hope, and Charity, else Masonry

will be a failure. The Brotherly Life may be difficult, but it is none the less needful. Our faith in
another may be repelled, or even shattered—what
then?

Nothing in Life is sadder than the pitiful moral
breakdowns of good men, their blunders and brutalities. Who knows his own heart, or what he
might do under terrible trial or temptation? Often
enough qualities appear or emerge, of which neither
the man himself nor his friends were aware, and
there is a moral wreck. Some "defect of will or
taint of blood," some hidden yellow streak, some
dark sin shows itself, and there is disaster. A man
highly respected and deeply loved goes down suddenly, like a tree in a storm, and we discover under
the smooth bark that the inside was rotten. What
shall we do?

Of course, in cases of awful crime the way is plain,
but we have in mind the erring Brother who does
injury to himself, his Brother, or the Lodge. An
old Stoic teacher gave a good rule, showing us that
much depends on the handle with which we take
hold of the matter. If we say, "My Brother has
injured me," it will mean one thing. If we say,
"My *Brother* has injured me," it will mean another;
and that is what the Brotherly Life means, if it
means anything.

Every Master of a Lodge knows how often he is
asked to arraign a Brother, try him, and expel him
from the Fraternity. It is easy to be angry, and
equally easy to be unjust. If he is a wise Master,
he will make haste slowly. There is need of tact,
patience, and, above all, sympathy—since all men

are a little weak and a little strong, a little good
and a little bad, and anyone may lose his way, be-
fogged by passion or bewitched by evil. It is a joy
to record that Masons, for the most part, are both
gentle and wise in dealing with a brother who has
stumbled along the way. Masonic charity is not a
myth; it is one of the finest things on earth.

What shall we do? If we see a Brother going
wrong in Masonry, or in anything else—"spoiling
his work," as the old Masons used to say—well, we
must take him aside and talk to him gently, man
to man, Brother to Brother, and show him the right
way. He may be ignorant, weak, or even ugly of
spirit—driven by some blind devil, as all of us are
apt to be—and if so our tact and Brotherly kindness may be tested and tried; but more often than
otherwise we can win him back to sanity.

Have you heard a tale about a Brother, a suggestion of a doubt, an innuendo about his character,
some hearsay story not to his credit? If so, did
you stand up for him, ask for proof, or invite sus-
pension of judgment until the facts could be heard,
remembering that it is your duty, as a Mason, to
defend a Brother in his absence? Such things are
seldom said in his presence. Is it not fair to tell
him what is being said and learn his side of the
tale? If we fail in our duty in such matters, we
fail of being a true Brother.

When we have learned the truth and have to face
the worst, what then? Years ago we knew an old
Mason, long since gone to the Great Lodge, who
was chided by a Brother for continuing to trust a
man they both knew was taking advantage of the

kindness shown him. The old man replied: "Yes,
but you never know; I may touch the right chord
in his heart yet. He is not wholly bad, and some
day, perhaps when I am dead and gone, he will hear
the music and remember." And he did.

Hear the music? Ah, if we would hear it we
must listen and wait, after we have touched "the
right chord." And if the right chord is *in us* something in him will respond, if he be not utterly dead
of soul! If he does respond, then you will have
gained a friend who will stick closer than a Brother.
If he does not respond—and, alas, sometimes he
does not—then we must admit, with a heart bowed
down, that we have done our best, and failed. Some
inherent failing, some blind spot, has led him
astray, dividing him from us by a gulf we cannot
bridge.

So a Mason should treat his Brother who goes
astray. Not with bitterness, nor yet with good-
natured easiness, nor with worldly indifference, nor
with philosophic coldness; but with pity, patience,
and loving-kindness. A moral collapse is a sickness, loss, dishonor in the immortal part of man.
It is the darkest disaster, worse than death, adding
misery to guilt. We must deal faithfully but ten-
derly, firmly but patiently, with such tragedies.

It is facts such as these which show us what
Charity, in a far deeper sense than monetary gifts,
really means. It is as delicate as it is difficult, in
that we are all men of like passions and tempta-
tions. We all have that within us which, by a twist
of perversion, might lead to awful ends. Perhaps
we *have* done acts, which, in proportion to the

provocation, are less excusable than those of a Brother who grieves us by his sin. "Judge not, lest ye yourselves be judged."

Truly it was a wise saying, not less true today than when the old Greek uttered it long ago, *"Know thyself."* Because we do not know ourselves, it behooves us to put ourselves under the spell of all the influences God is using for the making of men, among which the Spirit of Masonry is one of the gentlest, wisest, and most benign. If we let it have its way with us, it will build us up in virtue, honor and charity, softening what is hard and strengthening what is weak.

If an erring Brother must be condemned, he must also be deeply pitied. God pities him; Christ died for him; Heaven waits to welcome him back with joy. He has done himself a far deeper injury than he has done anyone else. In pity and prayer and pain let our hearts beat in harmony with all the powers God is using for his recovery. "There remaineth Faith, Hope, and Charity; but the greatest of these is Charity."

THE RUFFIANS

A S every Mason knows, at the heart of our mysteries lies a legend, in which we learn how three unworthy Craftsmen entered into a plot to extort from a famous Mason a secret to which they had no right. It is all familiar enough, in its setting and sequence; and it is a part of his initiation which no Mason ever forgets.

In spite of its familiarity, the scene in which the Ruffians appear is one of the most impressive that any man ever beheld, if it is not marred, as it often is, alas, by a hint of the rowdy. No one can witness it without being made to feel that there is a secret which, for all our wit and wisdom, we have not yet won from the Master Builder of the world; the mystery of evil in the life of man.

To one who feels the pathos of life and ponders its mystery, a part of its tragedy is the fact that the great man, toiling for the good of the race, is so often stricken down when the goal of his labors is almost within his reach; as Lincoln was shot in an hour when he was most needed. Nor is he an isolated example. The shadow lies dark upon the pages of history in every age.

The question is baffling:—Why is it that evil men, acting from low motives and for selfish aims, have such power to throw the race into confusion and bring ruin upon all, defeating the very end at which they aim? Is it true that all the holy things of life—the very things that make it worth living— are held at the risk and exposed to the peril of evil forces; and if so, why should it be so? Why should precious values be so precarious?

If we cannot answer such questions, we can at least ask another nearer to hand. Since everything in Masonry is symbolic, who are the three Ruffians and what is the legend trying to tell us? Of course we know the names they wear, but what is the truth back of it all, which it will help us to know? As is true of all Masonic symbols, as many meanings have been found as there have been seekers.

It all depends on the key with which each seeker sets out to unlock the meaning of Masonry. To those who trace our symbolism to the ancient solar worship, the three Ruffians are the three winter months who plot to murder the beauty and glory of summer, destroying the life-giving heat of the sun. To those who find the origin of Masonry in the Ancient Mysteries of Egypt, it is a drama of Typhon, the Spirit of Evil, slaying Osiris, the Spirit of Good, who is resurrected, in turn, rising triumphant over death.

Not a few find the fulfillment of this oldest of all dramas in the life and death of Jesus, who was put to death outside the city gate by three of the most ruthless Ruffians—the Priest, the Politician, and the Mob. Which of the three is the worst foe of humanity is hard to tell, but when they work together, as they usually do, there is no crime against man of which they have not been guilty.

A few who think that Masonry, as we have it, grew out of the downfall of the Knights Templar, identify the three Assassins, as they are called in the Lodges of Europe, with three renegade knights who falsely accused the Order, and so aided King Philip and Pope Clement to abolish Templarism, and slay its Grand Master. A very few see in Cromwell and his adherents the plotters, putting to death Charles the First.

It is plain that we must go further back and deeper down if we are to find the real Ruffians, who are still at large. Albert Pike identified the three Brothers who are the greatest enemies of individual welfare and social progress as Kingcraft, Priestcraft, and the ignorant Mob-Mind. Together they conspire to destroy liberty, without which man can make no advance.

The first strikes a blow at the throat, the seat of freedom of speech, and that is a mortal wound. The second stabs at the heart, the home of freedom of conscience, and that is well nigh fatal, since it puts out the last ray of Divine light by which man is guided. The third of the foul plotters fells his victim dead with a blow on the brain, which is the throne of freedom of thought.

No lesson could be plainer; it is written upon every page of the past. If by apathy, neglect or stupidity we suffer free speech, free conscience, and free thought to be destroyed either by kingcraft, priestcraft, or the mob-mind, or by all three working together—for they are Brothers and usually go hand in hand—the Temple of God is dark, there are no designs upon the Trestle-board, and the result is idleness, confusion, and chaos. It is a parable of history, a picture of many an age of which we read in the past.

For, where there is no light of Divine Vision, the Altar fire is extinguished. The people "perish," as the Bible tells us; literally they become a Mob, which is only another way of saying the same thing. There are no designs on the Trestle-board, that is, no leadership—as in Russia today, where the herd-mind runs wild and runs red. Chaos comes again, inevitably so when all the lights are blown out, and the people are like ignorant armies that clash by night.

Of the three Ruffians, the most terrible, the most ruthless, the most brutal is the ignorant Mob-Mind, so easily inflamed, so hard to restrain, and working such havoc in its fury. No tyrant, no priest can reduce a nation to slavery and control it until it is lost in the darkness of ignorance. By ignorance we mean not merely lack of knowledge, but the state of mind in which men refuse, or are afraid, to think, to reason, to enquire. When "the great freedoms of the mind" go, everything is lost.

After this manner Pike expounded the meaning of the three Ruffians, who rob themselves, as they rob their fellow-craftsmen, of the most precious secret of personal and social life. A secret, let it be added, which cannot be extorted, but is only won when we are worthy to receive it and have the wit and courage to keep it. For, oddly enough, we cannot have real liberty until we are ready for it, and we can only become worthy of it by seeking and striving for it.

But some of us go further, and find the same three Ruffians nearer home—hiding in our own hearts. And naturally so, because society is only the individual writ large; and what men are together is determined by what each is by himself. If we would know who the Ruffians really are, we have only to ask:—What three things waylay each of us, destroy character, and if they have their way either slay us or turn us into ruffians? Why do we do evil and mar the Temple of God in us?

Three great Greek thinkers searched until they found the three causes of sin in the heart of men. In other words, they hunted in the mountains of the mind until they found the Ruffians. Socrates said that the chief ruffian is Ignorance—that is, no man in his right mind does evil unless he is so blinded by ignorance that he does not see the right. No man, he said, seeing good and evil side by side, will choose evil unless he is too blind to see its results. An enlightened self-interest would stop him. Therefore, his remedy for the ills of life is knowledge—more light, a clearer insight.

Even so, said Plato; it is all true as far as it goes. But the fact is that men do see right and wrong clearly, and yet in a dark mood they do wrong in spite of knowledge. When the mind is calm and clear the right is plain, but a storm of passion stirs up sediments in the bottom of the mind, and it is so cloudy that clear vision fails. The life of man is like driving a team of horses, one tame and the other wild. So long as the wild horse is held firmly all goes well. But, alas, often enough, the wild horse gets loose and there is a run-away and a wreck.

But that is not all, said Aristotle. We do not get to the bottom truth of the matter until we admit the fact and possibility—in ourselves and in our fellows—of a moral perversity, a spirit of sheer mischief, which does wrong, deliberately and in face of right, calmly and with devilish cunning, for the sake of wrong and for love of it. Here, truly, is the real Ruffian most to be feared—a desperate character he is, who can only be overcome by Divine help.

Thus, three great thinkers capture the Ruffians, hiding somewhere in our own minds. It means much to have them brought before us for judgment, and happy is the man who is wise enough to take them outside the city of his mind and execute them. Nothing else or less will do. To show them any mercy is to invite misery and disaster. They are ruthless, and must be dealt with ruthlessly and at once.

If we parley with them, if we soften toward them, we ourselves may be turned into ruffians. Good but foolish Fellowcrafts came near being intrigued into a hideous crime. "If thy right eye offend, pluck it out," said the greatest of Teachers. Only a celestial surgery will save the whole body from infection and moral rot. We dare not make terms with evil, else it will dictate terms to us, before we are aware of it.

One does not have to break the head of a Brother in order to be a Ruffian. One can break his heart. One can break his home. We can slay his good name. The amount of polite and refined ruffianism that goes on about us every day, is appalling.

Watchfulness is wisdom. Only a mind well tiled, with a faithful inner guard ever at his post, may hope to keep the ruffian spirit out of your heart and mine. No wise man dare be careless or take any chances with the thoughts and feelings and motives he admits into the Lodge of the Mind, whereof he is Master.

So let us live, watch and work, until Death, the last Ruffian, whom none can escape, lays us low, assured that even the dark, dumb hour, which brings a dreamless sleep about our couch, will not be able to keep us from the face of God, whose strong grip will free us and lift us out of shadows into the Light; out of dim phantoms into the life Eternal that cannot die.

ACACIA LEAVES AND EASTER LILIES

APRIL brings us to Easter Day—the festival of Memory and Hope. That a day in spring should be set apart in praise of the victory of Life is in accord with the fitness of things, as if the seasons of the soul were akin to the seasons of the year. It unites faith with life; it links the fresh buds of spring with the ancient pieties of the heart. It finds in Nature, with its rhythm of winter and summer, a ritual of hope and joy.

So run the records of all times. Older than our era, Easter has been a day of feast and song in all lands and among all peoples. By a certain instinct man has found in the seasons a symbol of his faith, the blossoming of his spirit attuned to the wonder of the awakening of the earth from the white death of winter. A deep chord in him answers to the ever-renewed resurrection of Nature, and that instinct is more to be trusted than all philosophy. For in Nature there is no death, but only living and living again.

Something in the stir of spring, in the reviving earth, in the tide of life over-flowing the world, in the rebirth of the flowers, begets an unconscious, involuntary renewal of faith in the heart of man, refreshing his hope. So he looks into the face of each new spring with a heart strangely glad, and strangely sad, too, touched by tender memories of springs gone by never to return, softened by thoughts of "those who answer not, however we may call."

Truly it is a day of Hope and Courage in the heart of man. Hope and Courage we have for the affairs of daily life; but here is a Hope that leaps beyond the borders of the world, and a Courage that faces Eternity. For that Easter stands, in its history, its music, its returning miracle of spring— for the putting off of the tyranny of time, the terror of the grave, and the triumph of the flesh, and the putting on of immortality. Man can work with a brave heart and endure many ills if he feels that the good he strives for here, and never quite attains, will be won elsewhere.

There is something heroic, something magnificent in the refusal of a man to let death have the last word. Time out of mind, as far back as we can trace human thought—in sign or symbol—man has refused to think of the grave as the coffin lid of a dull and mindless world descending upon him at last. It was so in Egypt five thousand years ago; it is so today. At the gates of the tomb he defies the Shadow he cannot escape, and asserts the worth of his soul and its high destiny. Surely this mighty faith is its own best proof and prophecy, since man is a part of Nature, and what is deepest in him is what Nature has taught him to hope.

For some of us Easter has other meanings than those dug up from the folklore of olden time. Think how you will of the lovely and heroic figure of Jesus, it is none the less His day, dedicated to the pathos of His passion and the wonder of His personality. For some of us His life of love is the one everlasting romance in this hard old world, and its ineffable tenderness seems to blend naturally with the thrill of springtime, when the finger of God is pointing to the new birth of the earth. No brother will deny us the joy of weaving Easter lilies with Acacia leaves, in celebration of a common hope.

The legend of Hiram and the life of Jesus tell us the same truth; one in fiction and the other in fact. Both tragedies are alike profoundly simple, complete, and heartbreaking—each a symbol not only of the victory of man over death, but of his triumph over the stupidity and horror of evil in himself and in the world. In all the old mythologies, the winter comes because the ruffian forces of the world strike down and slay the gentle spirit of summer; and this dark tragedy is reflected in the life of man—making a mystery no mortal can solve, save as he sees it with courage and hope.

Jesus was put to death between two thieves outside the city gate. The Master Builder was stricken down in the hour of his glory, his prayer choked in his own blood. Lincoln was shot on Good Friday, just as the temple of Unity and Liberty was about to be dedicated. Each was the victim of sinister, cunning, brutal, evil force—here is the tragedy of our race, repeated in every age and land, as appalling as it is universal, and no man can fathom its mystery.

Yet, strangely enough, the very Shadow which seems to destroy faith, and make it seem futile and pitiful, is the fact which created the high, heroic faith of humanity and keeps it alive. Love crucified by Hate; high character slain by low Cunning! Death victorious over Life—man refuses to accept that as the final meaning of the world. He demands justice in the name of God and his own soul. The Master Builder is betrayed and slain; his enemies are put to death—that satisfies the sense of justice. Jesus dies with a prayer of forgiveness on His lips; Judas makes away with himself—and the hurt is partly healed.

But is that all? On the Mount of Crucifixion, by the outworking of events, goodness and wickedness met the same muddy fate—is that the meaning of the world? The Master Builder and his slayers are alike buried—is that the end? Are we to think that Jesus and Judas sleep in the same dust, all values erased, all issues settled in the great silence? No, never! By the splendor of God, it is not true! In the name of reason it cannot be true, else Chaos were the crown of Cosmos, and mud more mighty than mind!

When man, by the insight and affirmation of his soul, holds it true, despite all seeming contradiction, that virtue is victorious over brutal evil, and Life is Lord of Death, and that the soul is as eternal as the moral order in which it lives, the heart of the race has found the truth. Argument is unnecessary; the great soul of the world we call God is just. Here is the basis of all religion and the background of all philosophy. From the verdict of the senses and the logic of mud, man appeals to the justice of God, and finds peace.

'Thou wilt not leave us in the dust;
  Thou madest man, he knows not why,
  He thinks he was not made to die;
And Thou hast made him; Thou art just.

With what overwhelming impressiveness this faith is set forth in the greatest Degree of Freemasonry, the full meaning and depth of which we have not begun to fathom, much less to realize. Edwin Booth was right when he said that the Third Degree of Masonry is the profoundest, the simplest, the most heart-gripping tragedy known among men. Where else are all the elements of tragedy more perfectly blended in a scene which shakes the heart and makes it stand still? It is pathetic. It is confounding. Everything seems shattered and lost. Yet, somehow, we are not dismayed by it, because we are made to feel that there is a Beyond—the victim is rather set free from life than deprived of it.

Without faith in a future life, where the tangled tragedies of this world are made straight, and its weary woe is healed, despair would be our fate. By this faith men live and endure in spite of ills. Its roots go deeper than argument, deeper than dogma, deeper than reason, as deep as infancy and old age, as deep as love and death. As we do not ask logic to prove the coming of spring, so there is no need that anyone argue in behalf of the faith—older than history—that the power which weaves in silence robes of white for the lilies, of red for the rose, will the much more clothe our spirits with a moral beauty that shall never fade.

But there is a still deeper meaning in the Third Degree of Masonry, if we have eyes to see and ears to hear. It is not explained in the lectures; it is hardly hinted at in the lodge. Yet it is as clear as day, if we have insight. The Degree ends not in a memorial, but in a manifestation of the Eternal Life. Raised from a dead level to a living perpendicular, by the strong grip of faith, the Master Builder lives by the power of an endless life. That is to say, Masonry symbolically initiates us into the Eternal Life here and now, makes us citizens of eternity in time, and bids us live and act accordingly. Here is the deepest secret Masonry has to teach—that we are immortal here and now; that death is nothing to the soul; that eternity is today.

When shall we become that which we are? When shall we, who are sons of the Most High, born of His love and power, made in His image, and endowed with His deathless life, discover who we are, whence we came, and whither we tend, and live a free, joyous, triumphant life which belongs of right to immortal spirits! Give a man an hour to live, and you put him in a cage. Extend it to a day, and he is freer. Give him a year of life, and he moves in larger orbit and makes his plans. Let him know that he is a citizen of an eternal world, and he is free indeed, a master of life and time and death— a Master Mason.

Thus Acacia leaves and Easter lilies unite to give us the hint, if not the key, to a higher heroism and cheer, even "the glory of going on and still to be"; a glory which puts a new meaning and value into these our days and years—so brief at their longest, so broken at their best; their achievements so transient and so quickly forgotten. Sorrows come, and heartache, and loneliness unutterable, when those we love fall into the great white sleep; but the Sprig of Acacia will grow in our hearts, if we cultivate it, watering it the while with our tears; and at last it will be not a symbol but a sacrament in the house of our pilgrimage.

> What to you is Shadow, to Him is Day,
>   And the end He knoweth;
> And not on a blind and aimless way
>   Thy spirit goeth.
>   The steps of Faith
>   Fall on a seeming void, and find
>   A Rock beneath.

SO MOTE IT BE

HOW familiar the phrase is. No Lodge is ever opened or closed, in due form, without using it. Yet how few know how old it is, much less what a deep meaning it has in it. Like so many old and lovely things, it is so near to us that we do not see it.

As far back as we can go in the annals of the Craft we find this old phrase. Its form betrays its age. The word *mote* is an Anglo-Saxon word, derived from an anomalous verb, *motan*. Chaucer uses the exact phrase in the same sense in which we use it, meaning "So may it be." It is found in the Regius Poem, the oldest document of the Craft, just as we use it today.

As every one knows, it is the Masonic form of the ancient *Amen* which echoes through the ages, gathering meaning and music as it goes until it is one of the richest and most haunting of words. At first only a sign of assent, on the part either of an individual or of an assembly, to words of prayer or praise, it has come to stand as a sentinel at the gateway of silence.

When we have uttered all that we can utter, and our poor words seem like ripples on the bosom of the unspoken, somehow this familiar phrase gathers up all that is left—our dumb yearnings, our deepest longings—and bears them aloft to One who understands. In some strange way it seems to speak for us into the very ear of God the things for which words were never made.

So, naturally, it has a place of honor among us. At the marriage altar it speaks its blessing as young love walks toward the bliss or sorrow of hidden years. It stands beside the cradle when we dedicate our little ones to the holy life, mingling its benediction with our vows. At the grave side it utters its sad response to the shadowy Amen which death pronounces over our friends.

When, in our turn, we see the end of the road, and would make a last will and testament, leaving our earnings and savings to those whom we love, the old legal phrase asks us to repeat after it: "In the name of God, Amen." And with us, as with Gerontius in his Dream, the last word we hear when the voices of earth grow faint and the silence of God covers us, is the old Amen, So Mote it be.

How impressively it echoes through the Book of Holy Law. We hear it in the Psalms, as chorus answers to chorus, where it is sometimes reduplicated for emphasis. In the talks of Jesus with His friends it has a striking use, hidden in the English version. The oft-repeated phrase, "Verily, verily I say unto you," if rightly translated means, "Amen, amen, I say unto you." Later, in the Epistles of Paul, the word Amen becomes the name of Christ, who is the Amen of God to the faith of man.

So, too, in the Lodge, at opening, at closing, and in the hour of initiation. No Mason ever enters upon any great or important undertaking without invoking the aid and blessing of Deity. And he ends his prayer with the old phrase, "So mote it be." Which is another way of saying: The will of God be done. Or, whatever be the answer of God to his prayer: So be it—because it is wise and right.

What, then, is the meaning of this old phrase, so interwoven with all our Masonic lore, simple, tender, haunting? It has two meanings for us everywhere, in the Church or in the Lodge. First, it is the assent of man to the way and will of God; assent to His commands; assent to His providence, even when a tender, terrible stroke of death takes from us one much loved and leaves us forlorn.

Still, somehow, we must say: So it is; so be it. He is a wise man, a brave man, who, baffled by the woes of life, when disaster follows fast and follows faster, can nevertheless accept his lot as a part of the will of God and say, though it may almost choke him to say it; So mote it be. It is not blind submission, nor dumb resignation, but a wise reconciliation to the will of the Eternal.

The other meaning of the phrase is even more wonderful: it is the assent of God to the aspiration of man. Man can bear much—anything, perhaps —if he feels that God knows, cares and feels for him and with him. If God says Amen, So it is, to our faith and hope and love, it links our perplexed meanings, and helps us to see, however dimly, or in a glass darkly, that there is a wise and good purpose in life, despite its sorrow and suffering, and that we are not at the mercy of Fate or the whim of Chance.

Does God speak to man, confirming his faith and hope? If so, how? Indeed, yes! God is not the great *I Was,* but the great *I Am,* and He is neither deaf nor dumb. In Him we live and move and have our being—He speaks to us in nature, in the moral law, and in our own hearts, if we have ears to hear. But He speaks most clearly in the Book of Holy Law which lies open upon our Altar.

Nor is that all. Some of us hold that the Word of God "became flesh and dwelt among us, full of grace and truth," in a life the loveliest ever lived among men, showing us what life is, what it means, and to what fine issues it ascends when we do the will of God on earth as it is done in heaven. No one of us but grows wistful when he thinks of the life of Jesus, however far we fall below it.

Today men are asking the question: Does it do any good to pray? The man who actually prays does not ask such a question. As well ask if it does a bird any good to sing, or a flower to bloom? Prayer is natural, instinctive, in man. We are made so. Man is made for prayer, as sparks ascending seek the sun. He would not need religious faith if the objects of it did not exist.

Are prayers ever answered? Yes, always, as Emerson taught us long ago. Who rises from prayer a better man, his prayer is answered—and that is as far as we need to go. The deepest desire, the ruling motive of a man, is his actual prayer, and it shapes his life after its form and color. In this sense all prayer is answered, and that is why we ought to be careful what we pray for—because in the end we always get it.

What, then, is the good of prayer? It makes us repose on the unknown with hope; it makes us ready for life. It is a recognition of laws and the thread of our conjunction with them. It is not the purpose of prayer to beg or make God do what we want done. Its purpose is to bring us to do the will of God, which is greater and wiser than our will. It is not to use God, but to be used by Him in the service of His plan.

Can man by prayer change the will of God? No, and Yes. True prayer does not wish or seek to change the larger will of God, which involves in its sweep and scope the duty and destiny of humanity. But it can and does change the will of God concerning us, because it changes our will and attitude toward Him, which is the vital thing in prayer for us.

For example, if a man is living a wicked life, we know what the will of God will be for Him. All evil ways have been often tried, and we know what the end is, just as we know the answer to a problem in geometry. But if a man who is living wickedly changes his way of living, and his inner attitude, he changes the will of God—if not His will, at least His intention. That is, he attains what even the Divine will could not give him and do for him unless it had been affected by his will and prayer.

The place of prayer in Masonry is not perfunctory. It is not a mere matter of form and rote. It is vital and profound. As a man enters the Lodge, as an initiate, prayer is offered for him to God in whom he puts his trust. Later, in a crisis of his initiation, he must pray for himself, orally or mentally as his heart may elect. It is not just a ceremony; it is basic in the faith and spirit of Masonry.

Still later, in a scene which no Mason ever forgets, when the shadow is darkest, and the most precious thing a Mason can desire or seek seems lost, in the perplexity and despair of the Lodge, a prayer is offered. As recorded in our Monitors, it is a Mosaic of Bible words, in which the grim facts of life and death are set forth in stark reality, and appeal is made to the pity and light of God.

It is a truly great prayer, to join in which is to place ourselves in the very hands of God, as all must do in the end, trust His will and way, following where no path is into the soft and fascinating darkness which men call death. And the response of the Lodge to that prayer, as to all others offered at its Altar, is the old, challenging phrase: So Mote it be.

Brother, do not be ashamed to pray, as you are taught in the Lodge and the Church. It is a part of the sweetness and sanity of life, refreshing the soul and making clear the mind. There is more wisdom in a whispered prayer than in all the libraries of the world. It is not our business to instruct God. He knows what things we have need of before we ask Him. He does not need our prayer, but we do— if only to make us acquainted with the best Friend we have.

The greatest of all teachers of the soul left us a little liturgy called the Lord's Prayer. He told us to use it each for himself, in the closet when the door is shut and the din and hum and litter of the world is outside. Try it, Brother; it will sweeten life, make its load lighter, its joy brighter, and the way of duty plainer.

Two tiny prayers have floated down to us from ages agone, which are worth remembering, one by a great saint, the other by two brothers. "Grant me, Lord, ardently to desire, wisely to study, rightly to understand, and perfectly to fulfill that which pleaseth Thee." And the second is after the manner: "May two brothers enjoy and serve Thee together, and so live today that we may be worthy to live tomorrow."

So Mote It Be.

PART II – SERVICE

"For the good of the Order"

THE WONDER OF MASONRY

I

ONE of the Unwritten Sayings of Jesus, picked up in a rubbish heap in Egypt, is as follows: "Let him that seeketh desist not from his quest until he hath found; and when he hath found, he shall be smitten with wonder; and when he hath wondered, he shall come into his kingdom, and coming into his kingdom he shall rest."

A great English critic said that there are two impulses by which men are governed: the impulse of acceptance—the impulse to take for granted and unchallenged the facts of life as they are—and the impulse to confront those facts with the eyes of inquiry and wonder. Men are of two kinds, according as they obey one or the other of these two impulses.

As Watts-Dunton goes on to point out, in the latter years of the eighteenth century it was the impulse of acceptance that held sway; and it was precisely those years that made the winter of English poetry, when Pope and Dryden shone like stars on a frosty night. Then came what he has called "the Renascence of Wonder," and we heard again the bird notes of spring, of Cowper and Burns, of Wordsworth and Coleridge, of Shelley and Keats.

139

In the same way, Masons may be divided into two classes: those who take Masonry as a matter of course, and those who confront it with the eyes of inquiry and wonder. Let it be said at once, a man may be content—as indeed many are—with the impulse of acceptance, and may live a Masonic life without reproach; but he will never feel the thrill of Masonry as one of the great romances of the world.

II

To some of us Masonry is more fascinating than any fairy story—a thing so wonderful that we can never think of it without astonishment. The very existence of such an Order, older than any living religion, in one form or another going back into a far time where history and legend blend, like the earth and the sky on the horizon, is a fact amazing beyond words. If its real story were tellable, it would make other romances seem flat and tame.

Deep in the heart of man is an instinct, if we may call it such, by which he feels that there are truths so high and faiths so holy that they are not to be trusted to men unless they are trustworthy, lest the most precious possessions of humanity be lost or debased. Out of this feeling grew the idea and practice of initiation, as we see it in the Men's House, and trace it through all lands and races.

No matter what forms the old initiations might take, at the heart of it all, somewhere, one finds the rudiments of and resemblances to the great drama of the immortal life, showing that from earliest

time man defied death and refused to let it have
the last word. How this instinct for initiation, if
one may so describe it, linked itself with the art of
architecture, using its simple symbols to teach
moral truths; as if to teach man that he must build
up the eternal life within himself—how can one
think of such a fact without wonder and a strange
warming of the heart!

Yet there are brethren who seem to take it all
for granted, as a matter of rite and rote, and nothing more. They remind one of the letter of Horace
Walpole written from Florence: "I recollect the
joy I used to propose to myself if I could but once
see the Great Duke's Gallery: I walk in it now
with as little emotion as I should into St. Paul's
Cathedral. The farther I travel, the less I wonder
at anything."

Truly those words tell a pitiful tale of a jaded,
blasé tourist who walked through ancient shrines
of beauty and prayer with sealed, unwondering
eyes. Yet more marvelous than any cathedral is
the story of the Builders, out of whose faith and
dream and skill the cathedral was born and built;
and it is Masonry that tells us who the builders
were, why and how they wrought, and how we must
be builders, too, of a House not made with hands.

III

To name the marvels of Masonry would require
many books, but two may be mentioned, and the
first is its anonymousness. Who made Masonry no
one knows; when and how it was made no one has

told us. Much is said about the "revival" in 1717, but back of that date lies a long history, only glimpses and fragments of which we glean. Neither author, nor date, nor locality is attached to it. It is a monument, not of an individual, but of a mighty and mysterious past—like a cathedral the names of whose builders are lost. The genius that produced it has been forgotten in the service rendered.

Today we sit in a lodge listening to a ritual, not knowing when, where, or by whom it was written. It is a lyric fragment detached from time and place; it has come down to us singing its way on the unrelated wings of time. Its anonymousness is a part of its power. It is universal; it is not of an age or a race, but of the world. Some one ought to write a book entitled *The Anonymous in Life,* though it would assuredly take many volumes to tell the story of the wonders wrought by unknown, unnamed pilgrims of the past.

Think how much of the Bible is anonymous. Who wrote the idyl of Ruth, with the color of the loveliest sky on it and the wine of the purest love flowing through it? Who wrote that sublime epic of the desert, in which Job struggles with the mystery of undeserved suffering, and discovers a new dimension of faith in God? Who wrote the Epistle to the Hebrews, one of the most refined and gracious books of the New Testament? Origen said long ago, "No one knows but God."

Anonymousness takes all the egotism out of genius, gives absolute disinterestedness, converts the particular into the universal, and burdens it with a beauty and pathos, a dignity and nobility, which belong to humanity; as if the very soul of the race spoke to us, as the organ of the Infinite, instructing us, illuminating us. What Goethe said is true:

> But heard are the Voices,
> Heard are the Sages,
> The Worlds and the Ages.

How much of Masonry is anonymous! We do not know who is speaking to us. Their names are lost, like autumn leaves long fallen into dust. Like us, they were pilgrims and had to pass on. Yet what a legacy of inspiration and instruction they left us for our guidance on the old-world human road. They told us what they had learned by living, leaving their marks on the walls and arches of the Temple; and the rest is silence.

IV

Who can tell how, through long ages of ignorance, in the midst of bigotries and brutalities unbelievable—when the greatest crime was not murder, but thinking—our gentle Masonry kept its wise and good and beautiful truth, its mysterious largeness of mind and its tenderness of heart—the more one thinks of it all the more the wonder of it gathers and grows! In ages of intolerance, Masonry was not only tolerant but free, fraternal, gracious, seeking a bond of unity among those kept at a distance by old debates!

Surely he is a strange man, and no poet at all, who can think of the simple, kindly, fraternal wisdom of Masonry, and its spirit and art of brotherliness in ages of feud and fanaticism, when sect was set over against sect,—some of them small enough to be insects,—and men bandied bitter words, and even burned each other at the stake, and not feel a profound impulse of thanksgiving for sanity in the midst of insanity, mingled with a sense of the wonder of it all. Say what you will, there is something astonishing in Masonry, not only in the romance of its history, but in the mysterious largeness of its mind, no less than in wise tolerance in an intolerant age.

With what infinite patience those old teachers waited, with what skill and strategy they worked, to make and keep the lodge free from the things that divide men into cliques and sects, preserving for a better, brighter day truths so precious and a spirit which is the very breath of God. They knew the meaning of the words of Morley, which Olive Schreiner made the motto and title of her unfinished story: *"From man to man nothing matters but a boundless charity."*

A noble teacher, whose latter years were full of the most atrocious suffering, hammered out these words: The great secret of life is to find in ourselves and in God that which will enable us to endure and triumph over anything that life or death can do to us. Some call it religion; others call it by other names. No matter; he who finds it has found the pearl of great price. Is this the secret of Masonry?

V

"That's what it *is* really," said Burges, in the Kipling story, "In the Interests of the Brethren"—a story to break the heart, and mend it. "When I think of the possibilities of the Craft at this juncture, I wonder—" He stared into the fire.

"I wonder, too," said the Sergeant-Major slowly, "but—on the whole—I'm inclined to agree with you. We could do much with Masonry."

"As an aid—as an aid—not as a substitute for religion," the clergyman snapped.

"Oh, Lord! Can't we give Religion a rest for a bit," the Doctor muttered. "It hasn't done so—I beg pardon all around."

"Kamerad!" the wise Sergeant-Major went on, both hands up. "Certainly not as a substitute for a creed, but as an average plan of life."

Yes, platitudes or no platitudes, it does square with what every body knows ought to be done; and to do it we need such a Lodge of Instruction as that of which the story tells, attached to Faith and Works Lodge. Truly we need to know more about Masonry in order to do more with it. The Sergeant-Major was right: *We could do much with Masonry.*

THE OLDEST SYMBOL OF MAN

NEVER were truer words than those of Goethe in the last lines of *Faust*, and they echo one of the oldest instincts of humanity: "All things transitory but as symbols are sent." From the beginning man has divined that the things open to his senses are more than mere facts, having other and hidden meanings. The world was close to him as an infinite parable, and everything was so made as to convey a sense of doubleness, of high truths hinted in near-by things. No smallest thing but has its skyey aspect, which his quick-sighted thought and fancy sought to surprise and grasp.

Let us confess that man was born a poet, his mind a chamber of imagery, his world a gallery of art. Nor has he been able, despite his utmost effort, to strip his thought of the flowers and fruits which cling to it, withered though they often are. As a fact, he has ever been a citizen of two worlds, using the scenery of the visible to make vivid the realities of the world unseen. What wonder, then, that trees grew in his fancy, flowers bloomed in his faith, and the victory of spring over winter gave him hope of life after death, while the sun and the great stars invited him to "thoughts that wander through eternity." Such is the fact, and even the language in which it is stated is a dictionary of faded metaphors, the fossil poetry of ages ago.

Symbol, then, was the first form of human speech, as it is the last, for our highest thought, not less than the dim groupings of the earliest thinker, must needs be in parables and pictures. If only this fact had been realized, how many black and bitter pages of history would never have been written. Alas, men mistook the symbol for the reality, and set about by force to make others think in the same way. Thus the poetry of faith, frozen into hard dogma, lost its beauty and power, and men went to war about words. Our dogmas, did we but know it, are only picture-conceptions of truths, parables attempting to interpret and express a great object of insight, not decrees dictated by absolute truth. Losing the faith of poetry, men forget that creeds are but symbols and that charity is the soul of religion. As Carlyle, who was tolerant of men but intolerant of ideas other than his own, said:

By Symbols is man guided and commanded. He everywhere finds himself encompassed with Symbols, recognized as such or not. The Universe is but one vast Symbol of God; nay, if thou wilt have it, what is man himself but a Symbol of God? Is not all that he does symbolical; a revelation to sense of the mystic God-given force that is in him; a gospel of freedom, which he, the Messiah of Nature, preaches, as he can, by word and act? Not a hut he builds but is the visible embodiment of a thought, but bears visible record of invisible things; but is, in fact, symbolical as well as real.

Few studies are more fascinating than to look into the signs and symbols of primordial man. There you will find, often in startling foregleam, the beginning of every philosophy man has wrought out in history; for the story of thought seems but an elaboration and exposition of what man felt and hinted in his myths and symbols in the hush and awe of the morning of the world. Even Bergson, if his genealogy were traced, is only giving formal and reasoned statement of an insight as old as human thought. For this reason the old emblems of the race are rich in prophetic beauty and suggestion, and he who cares to know the truth will not pass them by. Also, certain symbols are as universal as they are ancient, and betray not only the comradeship of men, in the search for truth, but the unity of the human mind.

Some of these symbols take us back to an antiquity so remote that we seem to be walking in the shadow of prehistoric time. Of these, the mysterious Swastika is the oldest, the most universal, and one of the most eloquent. As much a talisman as a symbol, it has been found on Chaldean bricks, among the ruins of the city of Troy, on Hittite remains, in the cave-temples of India, on Roman altars and Runic monuments of Britain, in China and Peru, and among the burial-grounds of the American Indians. Akin to the Swastika, if not an evolution from it, was the Cross, made forever holy for us by the highest heroism of love. When man climbed up out of the primeval night, with his face to heaven upturned, he had a Cross in his hand. Where he got it, why he held it, and what he meant by it, no one knows. Itself a paradox, its arms pointing to the four corners of the earth, it is found carved on altars, coins, and tombs wherever man has lived. Ages before our era, among the cliff-dwellers, the Cross seems to have been a symbol of life. More often it was an emblem within a circle, which ends not nor begins—the type of eternity. Hence the Ank Cross of Egypt, scepter of the Lord of the Dead who never die.

What does the Swastika mean? Of the many interpretations of the symbol, two appeal to me as both beautiful and true. The first is suggested by the wife of Watts the artist, in his book *The Word in the Pattern,* where she traces it back to an old Sanskrit word meaning *It is well.* As such, she holds it to have been a sign indicating that while "the maze of life may bewilder, a path of light runs through it. *It is well* is the name of the path, and the key to life eternal is in the strange labyrinth for those whom God leadeth." That is to say, the first adventure of the human mind met with the discovery that life is good, and of that first faith, which may well be the last, the Swastika was a symbol. Hence the air of genial, joyous, courageous comradeship which clings to it, making it a talisman of good luck, of good heart, of good hope for the mysterious journey of man. Facing the world, man tried to read the riddle of things, and his intuitive insight taught him that love is at the heart of life!

Not unnaturally, then, the Swastika became not only a token of the beneficence of life, but a sign, a signal, whereby man wished his fellow good hap along the human way. Now a wish, when it is given wings by the will, becomes a prayer, for one of the oldest meanings of the word "prayer" is that it is a wish directed Godward. Canon Mozley has a remarkable sermon on *The Strength of Wishing*, in which he points out that the Bible teaches us that if a man wishes for any great spiritual gift, sooner or later the gift will be his, provided it be the supreme wish of his heart. That was what Emerson meant when he said that all men pray, and that every prayer is answered after its kind; therefore be careful what you pray for. Because the will is always sending out requests to the universe, all the powers of your being gather force to accomplish your desire. That is, our supreme wish demands of life what we want, and life sends it.

For all men live by faith, whether they are aware of it or not—only, alas, too often they have faith in the wrong things. Thus we have a facile faith in the power of misfortune, or calamity, or sorrow to crush the mind and paralyze the soul. That is faith, but faith in an error, and it needs to be changed to faith in the might of the soul to triumph over the calamities that come up against us. Or a man may have a great faith in the power of money, and take every advantage of his fellows, by fraud and lying, to secure his ends. That is faith misdirected, turned awry, perverted. He will not believe those who tell him that such a faith is folly, and he will be the loser and not the gainer by it, and that it will end in ruin. If men had that kind of faith in the truth, it would be easy to set things right in this world. Everything depends, not only upon how a man believes, but what he believes,

what idea of life he lays to heart and acts upon—
for that is ever his real religion.

Truly, the old Swastika may teach us something
which we need to lay to heart and never let slip
from us. Once a man has learned the truth that, at
heart, and no matter what may come, life is good,
there will be a still singing in his soul along the
dusty way. As Coleridge said, in his *Aids to Reflection*, if you would restore an old truth to its first
lustre, translate it into action. Now the Swastika
asks us to act upon the insight that life is sweet and
sane and true, and that it will show itself to be so.
Whoso does this will find that path of light running through the maze of things, and, if he will
follow it, he will be led out of the labyrinth. Like
the little girl in *The Servant in the House*, who had
such firm faith in wishing, his supreme wish will
come true at last, and his prayer will be answered.
By this law, those who live for eternal things come
to know the eternal life, even while they walk on
the dim shores of time.

There is, however, yet another truth hinted to us
by the ancient Swastika. Others hold it to have
been an emblem of the Polar Star whose stability
in the sky, and the procession of the Ursa Major
around it, so impressed the olden world. Men saw
the sun rise at dawn and vanish at dusk. They beheld it journeying across the heavens every day in
a slightly different track, then standing still, as it
were, at the solstice, and returning on its path.
They saw the moon changing not only its orbit,
but its size and shape and time of appearance.
Only the Polar Star remained fixed and stable, and

it is no wonder that it became a light of assurance and the foot-stool of the most high. They knew what Whittier felt when he wrote the lines:

> Yet, in the maddening maze of things,
>   And tossed by storm and flood,
> To one fixed trust my spirit clings;
>   I know that God is good!

Everything always in flux, sun and moon and stars ever on the march, the early men saw only one fixed point of light in the heavens. Of that faithful star and what it taught them of the changeless amid the ever-changing, the Swastika was the symbol. It is thus that the Swastika, by its very shape, represents rotation and rest, change and stability, motion and peace. It is a revolving cross, its arms turned to flanges, and as such forms the Cross within a circle—emblem of a still center of light in the rush and whirl of life. So then, amidst all the thunder of silent, ceaseless change, and the ebb and flow of things, there is something fixed and abiding, fixed even in its motion—something to which the heart may anchor hope. That is not less a need today than it was to the first men who watched the sky for a token of sure and steadfast faith; the more so just now when Bergson is telling us anew that life is motion, a stream ever flowing and never at rest. It sings in our sweet hymn of eventide, with its high, pathetic prayer:

> Oh Thou who changest not,
>   Abide with me.

If now we join these two truths together, the faith in the sanity and sanctity of life with the assurance of a reality that abides through all change, we have a basis for life and love and hope. It is no doubt true, as a poet has well said, that "God never does nor suffers to be done, but that you would yourself, could you but see the end and all events as well as He." But, having this sure word of faith wrought into the pattern of the world, we do not ask to see the distant scene. Our eyes are too dim and our minds too frail to follow, much less to comprehend, the vast sweep of destiny and all its intricate details. One step is enough, knowing that, while we cannot see all the way, there is ever a path through the labyrinth and a Kindly Light to lead us. Of this assurance the Swastika is the oldest emblem, telling us by what faith man dared to live in the morning of the ages, and never yet have we found a better, wiser, truer trust. No wonder he carved this symbol on his temples and his tombs, aye, even upon his coins and tools, for it is a faith to take with us into the marts of trade and amid the din and litter of our labor, not less than in the place of prayer.

Also, the Swastika is a sign of the road, left by those who passed before, wishing us good luck in the great quest in which all men are engaged. From of old this tradition of an age-long quest has come to us, taking many forms and phrases, yet ever the same, and having these things in common. First, the sense of a great loss which has befallen humanity, by which the race is made a pilgrim host of seekers. Second, the intimation that what was lost still exists somewhere in time and the world, albeit deeply hidden. Third, the faith that ultimately it will be found and the vanished glory be restored. Fourth, the temporary substitution of something less than the best, though never in a way to adjourn the quest. Fifth, and more rarely, the felt presence of that which was lost under veils and symbols close to the hands of all. Whether it be the Holy Grail, or a Lost Word, or the unfinished design of a Master-Builder; the pilgrimage of the Wandering Jew, or a journey to fairyland in search of *The Blue Bird;* it is always and everywhere the same. These are but so many symbols of the truth that men are made of one blood and born of one need; that they should seek the Lord and find Him. And evermore the Swastika wishes us good luck both in the seeking and the finding, of which it is itself at once a token and a prophecy.

Surely it is no mere fancy to link this oldest of all emblems with the great Cross outside the city gate, which has come to be, and rightly so, the supreme symbol of the race. He who suffered there, by a paradox deeper than we can fathom, by His very suffering made it a stroke of good luck for us to be alive in a world where love rules, Himself the answer to the eager, expectant aspiration of the ages, and the fulfillment of the highest dream of humanity. At first it may seem a far cry from the Ank Cross of Egypt to the Cross of Christ, but it means much to realize how deeply that Cross is rooted in the need and nature of man, and how eternal it is. He also is the day-star from on high, fixed forever in the sky of our faith and hope, stable amidst the mutations of thought and time; the path of light through the dim labyrinth of this world, and the key to the eternal life for those whom God leadeth.

There are those who affirm, with Browning, that since God is in His heaven, all is well with the world. That is, in so far, true, but it is not the whole truth by many leagues. God is not only in His heaven but in His earth, in all, over all, through all; but it is a daring optimism, if not more facile than daring, that can affirm, in face of the dark tragedies all about us, that all is well with the world. There are others who, taking heavy toll of dark fact, often feel, or fear, even when they do not affirm, that all is ill. No; there is nobler, ampler vision which, forgetting no darkest fact, sees through the shadow into the life and destiny of things, and dares to trust and say, not that all is well, nor yet that all is ill, but that all shall be well.

Every tangle will be untangled, at last, and every riddle unraveled. To this lofty and serene faith great souls come in the end, as Shakespeare did in *The Tempest*, after many heart-aches, many battles and bruises, and by its grace they sing their song of victory. In this faith Socrates died, affirming that no harm can come to a good man in this life or after death. Even so, "say ye to the rightous that it shall be well with him, for we have seen His star in the East."

THREE THINGS I KNOW

THREE times in my life a vision has visited me, each time more vividly than before. Each time it has come at the end of an hour of inner struggle and crisis, as if to light up a dark perplexity and show me the one way to go. No doubt such visions are the focus and glowpoint of much that has been going on in us below the surface of thought; and if that is their source, it is also their sanction and power.

Always it is a vision of an old gray cathedral, in the form of a Cross, stately, imposing, piteous, a shrine of faith and fellowship, and withal delicately poised as if it had come down from above instead of being built up from below. It is Gothic in its majesty and mystery, the form of architecture created and glorified by the genius and history of Freemasonry, at once its achievement and its monument; the noblest form of art, embodying the aspiration of humanity the while it makes God eloquent upon earth.

How stately and awe-inspiring it is in my vision —the lift of its pillars, the leap of its arches, its glorious dome—and to the ear of the mind melodious with a Voice that cannot be forgotten when once it has been heard. The Chancel and the Altar are invisible, not in darkness but in a blinding light

—dark with excess of light, as of one whose Presence is an Altar. There is "no Face, but the sight of a sweeping garment, vast and white"; and yet, while no Voice reaches me adown the aisle, somehow I know Who the Speaker is and what He is saying. Once again, in a framework of Gothic glory, He is speaking the words that He spoke of old, on the mountain and beside the sea; words of eternal life which defy time.

Hardly less wonderful is the audience gathered under that high and hospitable roof, the most extraordinary assembly of which any man ever dreamed. The mighty prophets of the elder world are there, the way-showers of mankind: Moses, the moral law-giver of the race; Confucius, who dreamed of the Superior Man; the all-pitiful Buddha, whose religion is the most majestic symphony of melancholy in the whole compass of human history. Socrates, the father of philosophy, is there, alongside Plato, the angel-minded idealist, and Aristotle, the father of science—patient, exact investigator who anticipated, in flashes of insight, so much of what has been verified later. Prophets and Apostles are there, Isaiah with his golden voice, the Saints and their shining company, and others whose presence surprises me, Voltaire, Goethe, and Hume. The finely chiseled profile of Emerson is distinct—what a company it is!

Such is my vision, at once a consummation and a consecration; and its crowning fact is that while the Speaker utters once more, with that voiceless voice, the truths which are the Magna Charta of the spiritual life of mankind, I see all those gathered in the cathedral nodding assent and saying, each in his own heart, Amen, Amen! Some day, perhaps, by the mercy of God, if I am counted worthy, it may be more vivid still, and some tone of that Voice may echo in my ears and become a melody in my heart.

So far a vision, and what does it mean? It is a vision of unity, embracing the ends of the earth and the limits of history, all religions and all races, looking backward and forward; and out of it have grown certain convictions which, like the rock ribs which hold the earth together, hold my life. First of all, religions are many but religion is one, perhaps we may say one thing—a Divine Life in the soul of man, underflowing the thickest ice of theory. All just men, all devout men, all spiritually minded men are everywhere of one religion, and all are trying to say the same thing, each in his own tongue, with his own accent and emphasis; the speech of each colored by his environment and the degree of his spiritual development. All are participators in one common spiritual life, which they seek to interpret.

Such a conviction makes me utterly indifferent to the small things which divide men into different religions and sects. In the light of my vision there is only one Church, universal and eternal, and all good men belong to it. The devout life is the same, albeit differently phrased, in Plutarch and Spinoza, in Francis and Channing. What Solomon called Wisdom, and Plato Justice, and St. Paul Charity are one and the same virtue, the treasure of all and the consecration of each. The different religions—

and, by the same fact, the various Churches—to me are like so many rooms in one Home of the Soul, and I walk from room to room in my Father's house. Wherever men seek righteousness and lift up hands in prayer, I am at home. No matter what the name of the temple may be, where Love is there God is, because God is Love, and the Religon of Love is the one external gospel. Such an attitude is no mere blur of sentiment in which truth is lost in a mist. Rather, it is a vivid sense of the higher unity of things which differ, and of the depths where humanity is one in its nature and need, as truth is one in its light and liberty.

My second conviction is that all good men everywhere, all men seeking goodness, are trying to do the same thing. Jesus saw this when he said, "Those who are not against us are for us"; meaning that all workers for the good are His helpers. Good men may differ as to method, but their motive is the same—to refine the faith of humanity, to exalt its mind, to purify its spirit, to build it up in righteousness. Above all seekers after goodness shine the same starry ideals. If Confucius speaks of the Superior Man, he means what we mean by the Christian Man. That is to say, there is one great moral enterprise in the world, and all good men are partners in it. Such a faith is a profound consolation, in that it brings the reinforcement of fellowship to those who follow lonely trails and stand for the ideal against all odds. It is both an inspiration and a consecration to know that we are not alone in our struggle for the good. It gives us patience and power.

Of these two convictions is born another, and that is the necessity of fraternity, since the great things can only be done together, by a united effort. Hence my deep interest in all forms of togetherness, in the Church and in the Lodge, and my longing to see men learn the art of co-operation. The great cathedrals were not built by one man, or even by one architect, but by a fraternity working in harmony, employing every gift in the service of one vision and plan. Not otherwise may we hope to build a better world order, in which the rule of moral reason shall overcome bigotry and brutality. Take, for example, war, which must be abolished if civilization is to endure. It is not necessary to get away from human nature in order to abolish war. No; it is only necessary to get man away from a false and foolish idea. What power can do it?

Pestilence, famine, war, these three; but the worst of these is war. Science has killed one pestilence after another, and they lie like dead snakes by the side of the road. Swift intercommunication makes it possible to send relief from one part of the world to another in time of famine. Only religion can put an end to war. Only a creative and co-operative spiritual life—renewed, united, sagacious, sacrificial—can kill the spirit of strife in the hearts of men and make war impossible. It will take the whole power of religion to do it. A petty sectarianism is utterly futile. It can be done, it must be done; to doubt it is to deny the reality of God, the rule of reason, and the power of the moral ideal over the life of man.

But I am thinking today of that Gothic Cathedral —stately and lovely in my vision—uplifted by the art and skill of Freemasonry, as a framework of fellowship and an altar of faith: its pointed arches prophetic of the expectation of man, its vistas like forest aisles, its towers a nesting-place of dreams. It is the great landmark of Masonry, the design upon its trestle-board, the end and aim of all its labor. It is also a parable of the service of Masonry to the faith of man. As of old it built the cathedrals, so, today, it toils to build a shelter for the holy things of man, where religion may grow and be glorified. For, while Masonry is not a religion, it is none the less a friend of all benign faiths, seeking to lay the foundations of the "religion in which all men agree." What are those foundations?

Three things I know about Freemasonry, not much else, though I have studied it for twenty years and more. It rests upon three fundamental facts, the first of which is that *man was made for righteousness*. No man can be a man, much less a happy man, until he is a righteous man. All evil ways have been tried often, with the same result—defeat, blight, tragedy. Byron in his wildest year wrote to Tom Moore: "Virtue, I begin to see, is the only thing that will do in this damned world." Exactly; the universe was built on that plan. The man who fancies that the moral order is a fiction, is taught the truth by terror and death, as Byron found, at thirty-seven, his manhood shriveled into a "sere and yellow leaf." Proofs could not be plainer if they were written in letters of fire in the blue sky.

Kant was right; the two overwhelming mysteries are the still depth of a starlit night and the awful whisper of the moral law in the soul of man. Explain it how you will, describe it as the echo within us of an old ancestral memory—that is only to push the mystery further back. The original bias toward righteousness remains to be accounted for. There is in man what John Woolman called "a stop in the mind," something which arrests us and compels us to pass moral judgment upon our thoughts and acts. What this voice is we may not know, but it cannot be hushed. It is here in my own heart. I did not create it. It commands me, whether I will or no. The fatalistic philosophy now in vogue may tell us that we are no more responsible for our acts than we are for the color of our eyes. It may be plausible, but every man knows that it is false.

Upon this foundation Masonry builds and finds it solid. It is the corner stone of all theology, the key to any understanding of life. Man was made for righteousness, and he cannot escape. Markham has a vivid little poem telling how a man, despairing of the good life, leaped wildly into the darkness of death—only to find himself face to face with the old duty and the old despair. There is no hope of happiness, here or hereafter, until we do justly and serve the good. To know that fact, and govern ourselves accordingly, is the beginning of wisdom and the first truth of religion.

Second, *man is made for man.* Fraternity is not a luxury, but a necessity and the very essence of religion, if it is to have any reality or worth. No man can attain to moral character, much less to spiritual personality, apart from his fellow men. Talent may develop in solitude, but character is the creation of fellowship. Here, again, Masonry builds upon a fact revealed in experience—that we are made for one another; our lives fit one into another like the stones of a temple. As we are taught in the parable of the Good Samaritan, if man will not help man in dire plight, his religion is vain, and his ritual mere rote without meaning. Nay, more; man cannot know the highest truth alone, but only in fellowship. It is by the practice of brotherhood that we learn to know God, the Father. My little poem may limp and falter, but it tells the truth:

It takes a father and a mother, two men and God
    To make a brother,
And show him the truth no one may know alone
    Or teach another.
The truth of God that makes man glad and free
    Is learned together,
On land and sea, in joy and woe, in sunny days
    And stormy weather.

Third, *man was made for God,* and his spirit is homeless and alone, even in the warmest human fellowship, until, at last, together, we find our source and peace in God, from whom we come and to whom we return in the last ineffable homeward sigh of the soul. The light that flashes across the soul in moral law and spiritual faith, like sparks ascending seek the sky, whence it came, reveals, if we have eyes to see, "the veiled kindness of the Father of man."

One of the greatest minds of any age tells us in a shining sentence whence we came, whither we go, and why we are restless and unhappy until we find our home: "Lord, Thou hast made us for Thyself, and our hearts are restless until they rest in Thee."

These things I know, and they are the foundations upon which Masonry builds the Cathedral of piety and prayer. To me, therefore, Masonry is a form of the Divine Life upon earth, a moral mysticism by which men of all types of temperament and training are drawn together and trained to be brothers and builders. The simplicity of its symbolism, the depth of its large, wise and kindly philosophy, no less than the strength of its fellowship, fill me with wonder and joy. It helps me to join hands with my fellows, and to do something, if it be only a little, before the end of the day, to make a gentler, wiser, kinder world.

MASONIC CITIZENSHIP

TWO texts from the Book of Holy Law tell us the two sides of citizenship, its earthly side and its ideal side. Both are from the words of St. Paul: "The powers that be are ordained of God"; and the last is equally striking "For our citizenship is in heaven." Taken together they mean that we are to live as citizens both of the State and of the Kingdom of Heaven, seeking to make the two one and the same. Such is in fact the challenge of all high citizenship—nothing else or less.

Elsewhere St. Paul speaks of two cities, the Jerusalem that is above and free, which is the mother of us all, and the old gray city on Mount Moriah, now in bondage to imperfection. One city is eternal, the other doomed to crumble and pass away. One is above, the other below—which is to teach us that human life is from above downward, and that our help is from God. Once we lose the vision of that fact, a shadow falls over the bright city of man, and the people perish.

If St. Paul had been an Englishman he would have said, "the London which is above and free"— the old mother city of a great race; the London of poetry, literature, and history disinfected and glorified. If he had been an American, he would have said "the Washington some of us have seen in our dreams as we looked upon the capitol, white and magnificent, in the moonlight, and saw as in a vision the fulfillment of the songs of our poets."

But St. Paul was a Hebrew who thought of the heavenly city in the imagery of the capital city of his native land. That is to say, his religion was patriotic and his patriotism was religious; the two being one creative passion, as they are everywhere in the Bible. Our patriotism should be religious in its depth, warmth, and purity; in its love of righteousness and its loyalty to the ideal. By the same token, our religion should be patriotic in its faith and faithfulness, in its trust in God and its sense of the sanctity of the social order.

When the Apostle spoke of "the powers that be," which he said are ordained of God, he referred to the Roman Empire—of which he was a citizen, and under whose protection he lived—a great empire of law established by the military genius of Julius Cæsar and the statesmanship of Augustus. It was almost the first attempt to organize civilization under law, its far-flung power making the world one, as its great stone roads brought the ends of the earth together. Surely, if St. Paul could speak of the Roman Empire as divinely ordained, we can say the same, and much more, for our republic, conceived in liberty and dedicated to the rights of man.

Back of the saying of St. Paul lies a profound philosophy of history, which sees that the will of God is worked out in the life of man only in so far as man works with that Eternal Will. The Roman Empire was the form which the will of God took in that far off time, because man was not ready or willing to receive a finer form—since God must wait for the developing capacity and wisdom of man. By the same fact, our republic is the form which the will of God takes in our age and land, because we are ready and willing to receive more of the eternal good will.

In other words, every people, every nation has as good a government as it deserves, or is ready to receive, whether it be an oligarchy, a monarchy, or a republic. For the same reason, we must strive by every means at our command—as individuals and in our collective life—to make our state more perfect, more responsive to the Divine will; and by so much do we make real progress. If our nation is founded upon the inalienable rights of man to life, liberty, and happiness, we must seek to make our life more abundant, our liberty more responsible, and our happiness more abiding. Such is the philosophy of Masonic citizenship, and it determines the methods by which our Craft of Builders works.

How can we make the Republic of Man the Kingdom of God, joining the streets of the earthly city onto the streets of the City that hath foundations, whose maker and builder is God? Not all at once, and only by heavenly methods. The trouble is that we are using earthly methods in trying to build the kingdom of heaven, and they do not work. We try to make men good by law instead of character, by repression rather than inspiration; and it cannot be done. God works from within outward, and only in His way can we build His kingdom on earth.

At first it seems a slow way, requiring a long time —and so it does—just as it takes a long time to grow a tree. But in all high matters the slow way is the quickest way, because it is the only way.

One danger of our time, by which the advance of righteousness is delayed, is the effort to do by force what can only be done by growth. Our statutory substitutes for character will not work. They fail and break down under pressure. Impatient of the slow process of moral unfolding, we seek to enforce righteousness. It always fails, and must fail in the nature of things, because it begins at the wrong end. Even the force of righteousness cannot make men righteous, else the power of God would have made men righteous long ago.

An example in point is the effort to make war a crime in the public law of the world. Suppose it were done; suppose a universal conference were called and a resolution passed outlawing war— what then? Does anyone imagine that it would put an end to war? Unfortunately no, unless, by some magic, the resolution went fathoms deeper and purified the spirit of man of the passions that make war. Moreover, by passing a law which runs so far ahead of the moral development of the race, we delay, if not defeat, the end in view.

All sane men, all human-hearted men hate war beyond all the power of words to tell. Especially do all Christian men hate it, because it is an outrage upon their faith and a crucifixion of their ideals. But it is of no use to deceive ourselves. Facts cannot be wished out of the way. And what are the facts? In the old Book which lies open

upon the Altar of the lodge, a question is asked in
respect to the matter in hand:

Whence come wars and fightings among you?
Come they not hence, even of your lusts that war
in your members? Ye lust, and have not; ye kill,
and cannot obtain. If ye have bitter envying and
strife in your hearts, glory not, and lie not against
the truth.

This wisdom descendeth not from above, but is
earthly, sensual, devilish. For where there is envying and strife, there is confusion and every evil
work. The wisdom that is from above is first pure,
then peaceable, gentle and full of mercy.

How far we are from such wisdom is revealed by
the fact that even our religious life, so called, is full
of strife, envy and confusion. Sect is set over
against sect, and the church which talks so elo-
quently about universal peace cannot keep the
peace in its own fellowship. Are such words cynical? Far from it; they merely state the facts which
we have to face. In the church, as in the lodge,
our ideals are made dim because we have not men
enough who will be loyal to them, serving them
with a high, disinterested courage and fidelity.

Nothing is easier than to save the world on paper.
A plan is made, a blue-print is made, but where are
the workmen to erect the temple? Only time, tact,
patience and a heavenly wisdom can train the
builders to build the House of God on earth. For
that reason our wise Masonry does not waste its
time with programs and projects of reform, but
spends all its influence in the making of men—

training them in moral insight, in the right use of
spiritual laws, in the fine art of manhood.

Manifestly, if we are ever to have the City of
God on earth it must first have citizens. The making and mending of men in the primary, basic work,
without which no dreams can come true and no
ideals can be wrought into reality. In using all its
time and influence in the making of men Masonry
is laying the foundations of the best things, and
the only basis of enduring progress.

Much as we love America—and some of us believe in America as we believe in God—we know
how far it is from being the kingdom of heaven.
If it is disfigured by racial rancor and religious
bigotry; if it is too much devoted to size, speed and
success; if materialism runs rampant, it is because
these things—these false ideals—are in our own
hearts; and so long as they are in our hearts they
will be in our life. Each man must begin with himself, and not by lecturing his neighbor. Long ago
our wise Emerson said:

> Things are in the saddle
> And ride mankind.
>   There are two laws discrete,
>   Nor reconciled—
> Law for man, and law for thing;
> The first builds town and fleet,
> But it runs wild,
> And doth the man unking.

Until we learn the law for man—the law of
values, of fellowship, of service, of working together
for the common good—as well as we have learned

"the law for things" in our amazing mastery of material things, we cannot make much advance toward fraternal righteousness. Where in all the world does man learn the "law for man" as he learns it in the lodge? For such teaching no better school was ever imagined, and in the kind of men it selects and trains Masonry renders its best and most far-reaching service to citizenship—making all sacred things more secure, all holy things more real.

Well does the writer know that what he is here saying will be regarded by many as old-fashioned, slow, and of little import. No matter; he also knows that some things abide amid all the chances and changes of life. Nay, more; unless we build in accordance with these old, stable, immutable laws of God, our house will not stand when the winds blow and the floods of folly beat upon it. Man has sought him out many inventions in earth and sea and sky, but he cannot invent a better way to manhood and the practice of brotherly righteousness than he is taught in the Volume of Sacred Law.

So, at least, one humble craftsman muses the while in the midst of motors, movies, and jazz, when reformers go to and fro in the earth seeking whom they may make good, and every kind of creed and cult cries itself hoarse, like a barker at a sideshow, offering some patent panacea for all the ills of mortal life. In these despites, he hears a still, small, authentic voice which tells us the truth:

He hath showed thee, O man, what is good; and what doth the Lord require of thee, but to do justly, to love mercy, and to walk humbly with thy God?

FREEDOM OF FAITH

IN AMERICA we are proud of the fact that Church is separate from State, and justly so. Our freedom of faith is our most precious heritage, a thing of priceless worth. Too often we take it for granted, forgetting what it cost and to whom we are indebted for it.

The right of each man to worship God in the way his heart loves best is so in keeping with the idea and spirit of Masonry, so much a part of its genius, that we need to celebrate it anew in this 150th year of our national life. If for no other reason, because both directly and indirectly our Craft had much to do with it.

Our fathers founded our Republic upon a new basis, reversing the whole history of mankind. Before that time a country without its national Church, with its official creed, was quite unknown. But America broke new ground, made a new adventure, which must be reckoned by far the most important since the Reformation, and even more far-reaching. Such a thing was not done without difficulty.

Even in Colonial times Church and State were one. In New England the ideal was a theocracy, a Church which included the State. In the South, if the State included the Church, they were none the less united. Religious liberty was almost unknown, except by those who defied the law and endured persecution to enjoy it.

Few realize that prior to the Revolution it was against the law not to go to Church. It was a crime not to baptize a child in the established Church. It was a crime to bring a Quaker into the colony, and there was a law on the statute books—though, happily, not enforced—that permitted the burning of heretics. Witches had been executed in New England; Quakers had been hung. Everybody was required to pay tithes to maintain the Church, and that regardless of their religious affiliations. Those who failed to do so were thrown into prison.

Smarting under these infringements on religious liberty, Jefferson led and Madison followed in the fierce struggle to separate Church and State. To Jefferson, more than to any other one man, we owe our liberty of faith today. The famous law which first forbade any religious tests for public office was written by Jefferson, and its principles were embodied in the first amendment of the national Constitution. The heart of that statue, couched in noble language, is as follows:

"We, the general assembly of Virginia, do enact that no man shall be compelled to frequent or support any religious worship, place, or ministry, whatsoever, nor shall be enforced, restrained, molested, or burthened in his body or goods, or shall otherwise suffer on account of his religious opinions or beliefs: but that all men shall be free to profess and by arguments to maintain their opinions in matters of religion, and that the same shall in no wise diminish, enlarge, or affect their civic capacities."

What seems a natural and inalienable right of man to us today, was a daring demand in those days. It is a curious fact that while Jefferson did not differ widely in his religious views from Franklin, Adams, and even Washington, he was singled out for the most savage attacks for his part in writing the above law, and for pressing for its passage in Virginia —and, later, in the nation. Throughout his life he was a target of bitter abuse, nor did it cease after his death.

Even the casual reader of the newspapers and pamphlets of that day knows how Jefferson was lampooned for his fight for liberty of faith. He was called a *sceptic,* an *infidel,* an *atheist*—names which had terrifying meanings in those days—all because he demanded that each man have the right to hold such religious faith as seemed to him right and true and good. So much our liberty of faith cost; against such odds the spirit of tolerance had to make its way.

The writings of Jefferson abound in allusions to his religious views, which he made no effort to conceal. They also show his familiarity with the Bible, in which he surpassed any leading man of his time, not excepting Franklin who was a student of it. The ethics of Jesus fascinated him. During his first term in the White House he found time to make a syllabus of the teachings of Jesus compared with the moral codes of other religions, in which he made out a strong case for the superiority of the ethics of Jesus. In 1816 he wrote to his friend Thompson of what he had been doing:

"I have made a wee little book, which I call The Philosophy of Jesus. It is paradigm of his doctrines, made by cutting the texts out of the book and arranging them on the pages of a blank book, in a certain order of time and subject. A more beautiful and precious morsel of ethics I have never seen. It is a document in proof that I am a real Christian, that is, a disciple of the doctrines of Jesus."

Yet this was the man denounced as an "atheist," and held up to scorn as an enemy of God and man, because he held that others had a right to disagree with him and yet enjoy the honors of citizenship. No wonder he wrote his confession of faith in the word: "I have sworn upon the altar of God eternal hostility against every form of tyranny over the mind of man." Ignorance and intolerance were the two enemies which he fought all his days, without truce.

From Paris he wrote to George Wythe in 1786: "Preach, my dear sir, a crusade against ignorance, establish and improve the law for educating the people." To that end he himself had founded the University of Virginia, in which there were no religious tests for professors or pupils. Students of theology were invited to attend and enjoy the lectures and the library. As he said: "By bringing the sects together and mixing them with the mass of other students we shall soften their asperities, liberalize and neutralize their prejudices and make the general religion a religion of peace, reason and sanity."

In his own life Jefferson was brought up in the

Church, and was a fairly regular attendant on its services. As an architect he planned at least one Church, and gave freely to the erection of others and to the support of public worship. A lover of the Bible, he gave freely to Bible societies. No one ever heard him use an oath, and his magnanimity was such that he placed a marble bust of his political antagonist, Hamilton, in the hall at Monticello. Such was the man who, dying, murmured with his last breath as he sank into sleep the old, beautiful Bible prayer: "Now lettest Thou Thy servant depart in peace."

While it has not been shown that Jefferson was a Mason, as was at one time thought, all Masons will honor in the Lodge, and in their hearts, the man to whom, more than to any other of the men who laid the foundation of our Republic, we are indebted for religious freedom—that is, for the glory of a free Church in a free country. For it was as much an emancipation for the Church as for the State, and it has been an unmixed blessing to both.

To have written the Declaration of political Independence was a great honor, but not a few will think it an even greater honor to have led in the achievement of religious independence. It closed a long and bloody chapter of history; it marked a new era, second only to that of the advent of Christ among men.

As has been said, Masonry had much to do with it, directly and indirectly. Directly in that the leaders with whom Jefferson worked and without whom he would have failed, were most of them

Masons. And indirectly by virtue of the fact that Masonry does its greatest work, not by laws and edicts, but by its teaching and influence.

If any one will read the Virginia statute on religious liberty, and the first amendment of the Constitution, along side the article on God and Religion in the Constitution of the Grand Lodge of England in 1723, he will discover that the spirit and purpose of all three documents are the same. The Masonic Constitution, written more than fifty years earlier, was one of the ancestors of the other statements.

Thus by our history, no less than by our Constitution and genius, Masons are pledged to keep Church and State separate, and to watch vigilantly every insidious effort to unite the two. Such efforts are always afoot, disguised in all sorts of ways, but we ought to be able to detect the wolf even when it wears the white robe of a lamb. It asks for clear thinking and a tireless vigil, but Masons will not fall asleep and let the work of our fathers be undone.

Just now the whole set of the old world is against the spirit and ideals of our Republic. Dictators strut to and fro, declaring themselves supermen born to rule their fellows. Heretofore the loss of political liberty has always been followed by a loss of religious freedom. The two go together, as our fathers joined them; and what God hath joined man must not put asunder.

THE GREAT CORNER STONE

MY BRETHREN, as you well know, a corner stone unites two walls and gives unity and solidity to a building, by joining and sustaining its many parts. It is the key-stone of the foundation. Everything depends upon it; everything proceeds from it. If the corner stone is faulty the structure is frail. Unless the corner stone is well and truly laid upon a solid base, the house will not be stable.

The Constitution of our Republic is the great corner stone of liberty and law in our nation. It was wrought out and laid down upon a bedrock of righteousness by wise and just men. Everything rests upon it. By it all liberty is regulated, all law tested. It unites many States into one nation, yet keeps the integrity of each. Truly it is the written will of God for our country, at once its foundation and its security.

Good work, true work, square work went into the making and laying of the great corner stone of liberty. It is square with the order of the world, in which liberty and obedience, justice and mercy, join, or neither is safe. It is true to the needs, duties and hopes of man, giving to each the right to life, liberty, and the pursuit of happiness, and the duty of allowing to others the same rights. Under its wise and benign power all may live, and live well, uniting individual initiative and social obligation.

As such it is a bulwark against autocracy and anarchy alike, against rule by the few and ruin by the mob. By its wise poise of power, representative but not ruthless, we have advanced thus far along the path of our history. Under its calm wisdom we map our path into the future, yet keep the treasure of a time-tried past. Upon it is built a "government of the people, by the people, and for the people," which "shall not perish from the earth." It unites the dead, the living, and those yet unborn into a community of memory, service and hope.

Gladstone said that our Constitution was the most wonderful work ever struck off at a given time by the brain and purpose of man. But it was not struck off. Back of it lay ages of experience, in which the race struggled for the rights of man. Out of that mountain of history, as out of a quarry, our Constitution was slowly wrought, in the face of difficulties and defiances which only a divine aspiration and determination in the heart of the race could have overcome. Faith cut it, truth shaped it, time polished it, making a chief corner stone ready for the builders.

To put it in our own imagery, the Magna Charta, the Bill of Rights, and the Habeas Corpus Act were like the Entered Apprentice Degree in the great initiation into free government. The Bills of Rights and Constitutions framed by various Colonies, and even the Declaration of Independence, may be called the Second Degree, in which Fellows in the sublime Craft of Freedom wrought brilliantly. At last, as the Master Degree, after the shadow of war, with its blood and fire and tears, came the Constitution, the final expression in a single document, in permanent and definite form, of the will of a free people. It is an august instrument such as man had never known before; no vain declamation but a grand affirmation, clear, concise, comprehensive, of the principles of organized liberty and just and wise law.

No wonder it has won the homage of mankind as the "last best hope of earth." It divided history into before and after, opening a new era. Washington wrote: "I can almost trace the finger of Divine Providence through those dark and mysterious days, which first led the colonists to assemble in convention, thereby laying the foundation for peace and prosperity." Hamilton, also a member of our Craft, was no less explicit: "The sacred rights of mankind are not to be rummaged for among old parchments or musty records. They are written as with a sunbeam in the whole volume of human nature, by the hand of Divinity itself. The establishment of a Constitution in time of profound peace by the voluntary action of all the people is a prodigy." With which agree all the great voices that echo through our history.

Like all true wisdom, our Constitution was, and is, a compromise between two widely different ideas of government, a balance between the extremes of oligarchy and democracy. Our fathers dreaded the madness of the many as much as the arts of the few. They were equally afraid of the despot and the mob. Their problem was to guard the rights of the States, and yet give the Federal government adequate power. The negotiations were often difficult, and were more than once saved from wreck by the tact, patience, and wisdom of Franklin, Dickinson, Sherman, and most of all Madison, who was called "the father of the Constitution." Two ideas were ever present in their minds, one that the people should rule, and the other that the will of the people should be carefully and deliberately expressed, not swayed by gusts of popular passion. As Madison put it, though every member of the Athenian Assembly had been a Socrates, the aggregate body would have been a mob.

The result of their labors was a Republic, not a democracy, as too few seem to realize. In a democracy, such as we see in Switzerland, the people make and administer the laws, which may be possible in a small country of intelligent and homogeneous population. What it means in a large country of mixed races has been shown us of late in Russia, where pure democracy ended in the worst kind of autocracy. In a Republic, what Washington called "the delegated will of the people," is vested in representatives elected by the people. The rank and mass of the people will not be bothered with the details of state, even when they are capable of dealing with them, as is shown in our time by the amazing neglect of the ballot. The wisdom of our fathers has been justified in ways too many to name.

Ours is a representative government, not a pure democracy, as we need to keep in mind, if only because, in recent years, the tendency has turned more and more toward democracy. As such it is hedged about with every kind of device to avoid hasty and ill-judged action, in order to protect the people from themselves, and yet to give expression to their real and considered will. As we look back over our history, we see this wise balance of power tipping now toward one extreme, and now toward another, always with bad results; and it behooves us to keep the poise, if we would keep our sanity which is our safety.

Of the Constitutional Convention, it may be truly said that a more remarkable assembly of men has never foregathered in history, anywhere or at any time. They were young men, for the most part, though men were deemed old earlier in those days than they are today. Madison was only thirty-six; Dayton of New Jersey twenty-one. As Masons, we have a right to be proud of the number and quality of the men of our Craft who sat in that conclave of the great. Washington who presided was of our Fraternity; and Franklin, whose quaint humor saved many a tense hour; and Hamilton, in whom genius and wisdom joined; as well as others. Indeed, it has been said that with a very few men out of the room, the Convention could have been opened on the Third Degree of Masonry.

Thus Freemasonry, in the formative days as in all the years of its story, influenced profoundly, creatively, the organic law of our Republic. How well the fathers wrought is shown by the fact that for sixty-one years, from 1804 to 1865, not a single amendment was added. In the five years following the Civil War, the 13th, 14th and 15th amendments were ratified. Then for forty-three years no other amendments were adopted, when a movement, vast as a flowing tide, to extend the idea and spirit of democracy, found expression in the 16th, 17th, 18th and 19th amendments. Just now the tide is ebbing, but it will no doubt return, in obedience to the law of ebb and flow. If we are true to our history and the genius of our Republic, we shall have a care to do nothing in haste, lest we injure a wise plan in order to make an immediate gain.

Let me tell a story, a true story, in order to point a moral. In a lumber camp in the West a group of radical lumber jacks—men from the ends of the land—were one evening discussing the sad state of the world, and especially the wickedness of the Government. They agreed, unanimously, that our Government is all wrong, if not actually rotten, a dirty, capitalistic conspiracy against the rights of the man who works. They said that it ought to be torn to pieces and made over again. Among them was a young minister, a missionary, who listened to their talk, and even drew it out at full length by the questions he asked. Finally, pretending to agree with their radical ideas, he wrote on a piece of paper the following, which he proposed as a basis of a just state:

"We, the people, in order to form a more perfect union, establish justice, insure domestic tranquillity, provide for the common defense, promote the general welfare, and secure the blessings of liberty to ourselves and our posterity, do ordain and establish this Constitution."

"That's the stuff! Hit 'em again," they yelled. "If we had a government built on that dope, every feller would have a square deal, and a chance to live a bit. Some head you got, Padre; go on and give us more."

"Listen, boys," said the Padre; "what I read is the preamble of the Constitution of the United States. If we tore everything to pieces and set out to make it all over, do you think we could do a better job?"

The missionary himself told me the story, adding that as he listened to the talk of the evening— earnest, passionate, and bitter—he was half inclined to agree with much of it, until he began to consider how a better state could be constructed. This led him to think of the Constitution, its wisdom and poise and justice, and the wonder of it dawned upon him like a revelation. He remembered the saying of Hamilton that it is of great importance, not only to guard against the oppression of rulers, but also to protect one part of society from the injustices of the other part. He recalled his very words:

"Justice is the end of government. It is the end of civil society. It ever has been, and ever will be pursued until it be obtained, or until liberty be lost in the pursuit."

As Lincoln put it, between those who will "let nothing alone" and those who will allow no change at all, there is a middle way of wise and cautious advance. He approved the praise of Burke for those men in public life who have "disposition to conserve and the ability to improve," adding that we must have not only the wish but the ability to improve, else we shall lose what we have while blunderingly trying to get what we want.

To defend, preserve, and obey the Constitution of our Republic is the first obligation of every citizen, as it is the first oath of every officer. To teach its history and meaning is the duty of school and church and lodge—making it the Bible of our Political Religion; and to observe its birthday ought to be a universal festival from end to end of the land.

THE GUNS OF '75

ONE hundred and fifty years ago! The Battle of Lexington was fought on April 19, 1775; the Battle of Bunker Hill on June 17. What emotions, what echoes, what old historic memories stir in our hearts as we remember those days and dates. When Lafayette held in his hand the musket which fired the first shot of the American Revolution, he exclaimed: "This is the alarm gun of liberty!"

To England the war was an episode; to us it is an epic. Time does not tarnish those events, nor distance dim the glory of days that tried the stuff of which men are made. All that America means, all that it has become, had its beginning at Lexington and Bunker Hill. It meant a new nation, built upon a new basis, with a new relation of Church and State, a new opportunity for mankind —the opening of a new era.

An oft-told story, taught us from our earliest years, it throbs like a drum-beat in our blood, like the echo of the foot-steps of God in time. Emerson said truly that the farmers who stood at Concord Bridge fired "a shot heard 'round the world." Its flash divided the records of man into before and after, and its echoes will never die while men love liberty and value the rights of man. It was the first act in a drama of history, but, somehow, it reads like a record of our Family Bible.

For history, in its great meaning, is more than a series of events. It is an unfolding of ideas, the fulfillment of a Divine purpose in time. Events do not stand alone. They are linked together by a thread of cause and effect, a law of seed-time and harvest. What went before explains what followed after. If we are to know the meaning of the events we remember today, we must go back of the immediate inciting causes to the facts and forces that lay behind. History is philosophy teaching by example; it is theology acted out.

Our sturdy forefathers who emigrated first to Holland, and then to America, bore with them the seeds of liberty. Those seeds, nourished by the wise tolerance of the Dutch, they planted in the fresh soil of the New World. They sought the New World in search of liberty of conscience and freedom of worship. Let us never forget that our independence was first religious, then political. Our democracy had a spiritual foundation, our republic a sacred origin. Having breathed the air of religious liberty, by a sure logic our fathers finally demanded the same liberty in political affairs. They would gladly help pay debts incurred partly in their behalf; but they refused to be taxed to that end, unless they were allowed to have a voice in shaping the policy of state. It was the old, high British ideal, forgotten by the motherland and defended by its sons.

The reigning King did not understand the Colonists. They were a long distance from the homeland, and no longer under the mystic spell which waits upon royalty. But they were loyal and law-abiding. As Franklin said, they were ruled "at the sole expense of pen and ink"; but they could not be coerced. One irritating act after another provoked anger, and at last alienation, until men in America began to hate the land which formerly they had loved. The Boston Tea Party, planned in old St. Andrew's Lodge, and carried out by Masons masked as Mohawk Indians, was the last straw. The tension tightened, until finally the tie of allegiance was broken and resentment flamed into revolt.

Early in 1775 news arrived that Parliament, in spite of the pleadings of Pitt, Burke and Fox, had rejected the petition of the first Continental Congress, declaring that "rebellion existed in America." It did, though it might have been averted, like nearly every war in history. On the night of April 18 troops were sent by General Gage to seize the powder stored by the Sons of Liberty at Concord, and to arrest as "traitors" John Hancock and Samuel Adams, who had taken refuge with Parson Jonas Clark at Lexington. They set out secretly, as they thought, not knowing how alert and watchful the patriots were, and how well organized.

Lanterns, hung out in the tower of the old North Church, flashed the signal far and wide, and Paul Revere and William Dawes rode through the night ahead of the troops led by Major Pitcairn, rousing the people and giving the alarm. When the British column reached Lexington they found a little company of "minutemen" drawn up on the village green, under command of Captain Parker, who had given the order: "Stand your ground. Don't fire unless fired upon. But if they mean to have war let it begin here." Major Pitcairn ordered the "rebels" to disperse, and they refused to move. A shot was fired, apparently without his order, then a volley, and a number of minutemen were killed and wounded. With a shout the British marched off to Concord, took what military stores they found, rifled some houses, and encountered a company of farmers.

Again the Colonists, under Major Butterick and Captain Davis, were ordered not to fire unless fired upon. In double file they crossed the bridge and waited, the young fifers playing the "White Cockade." When within a few yards of the bridge a shot fired by the British wounded one of their number; a volley followed and two were killed. Then the minutemen were ordered to fire—the first gun of the American Revolution—and the British began to retreat. As Emerson said in his Concord Hymn, April 19, 1836:

> By the rude bridge that arched the flood,
> Their flag to April breeze unfurled,
> Here once the embattled farmers stood,
> And fired the shot heard 'round the world.

By this time the whole countryside was aflame with anger and excitement. Men and boys came running, singly and in bands, and from behind hedges, trees and stone walls along the road to Boston, poured shot into the retreating British ranks, following them all the way until they were safe under the protection of their guns. Thus, without previous design, the war began, destined to change the history of the world. Small events, born of human blunder, become great by virtue of the ideas and influences back of them, and initiate vast movements. The fight on the village green and by the bridge was hardly more than a skirmish, but it was used by a Power other than human to institute the greatest Republic on earth.

The battle of Lexington shut the British up in Boston, then almost an island linked with the mainland by a narrow strip of sand beach. To the north lay the peninsula of Charlestown, on which were two hills, Breed's Hill and Bunker Hill. To the south Dorchester Heights overlooked the city. The American army grew rapidly, as men flocked in from all directions—ill-prepared in all save courage. On June 17 they began busily to fortify Bunker Hill, and the British attacked. Twice the redcoats stormed up the hill only to be hurled back. When they made their third desperate charge they won, because the Americans had used all the powder they had, and were forced to flee, leaving Warren, Grand Master of Masons, dead on the hill. Lack of preparedness lost the battle—a lesson never to be forgotten by those who are wise!

Yes, it is an old story, my brethren, as familiar to us as the alphabet; but it is a story that makes our hearts beat fast, in which our gentle Craft had an honorable part of which we have a right to be proud. It is the simple truth to say that our ancient Fraternity—faithful, wise, and heroic—presided in the birth-hour of our Republic, as it guards its sanctity today. There are those who would be-little its influence, but the facts stand. It was not an accident that Washington and most of his gen-erals were members of the Craft. The story of the War of the Revolution might have been very dif-ferent had not its leaders been bound together by the tie which Masonry knows how to weave be-tween men, making them brothers. Even Lafayette was not given a place of power until after he had been initiated in a military Lodge.

What followed we know as we know our family history. The genius of Washington, the dark days of Valley Forge, the crossing of the Delaware, the coming of Lafayette, the final scene at Yorktown, the Constitution, the far-flung Republic—it is a story and a tradition bequeathed to us in the mystic continuities of inheritance. America was born—the last great hope of humanity—created by the will of God and the heroism of man, and dedicated to the service of peace on earth and good will to men. As in its origin, so in its history, our Republic is a fraternal symposium, in which many races are being built together into one community—an en-terprise the full meaning of which we do not yet realize.

If we celebrate our beginnings at Lexington, Bunker Hill and Yorktown, we do so with no ill will toward the motherland against which our fathers fought, wresting their liberties from an obstinate King and a truckling Parliament. Since then, in the greatest of all wars, Americans have fought side by side with Britons, in an hour of common peril and high resolve, for the same principle for which our fathers fired "the shot heard 'round the world!" The old feud long since gave place to friendship, to deepen and maintain which is the first duty of thoughtful men on both sides of the sea.

Yet we do affirm the uniqueness of America, and we are bound by ties of blood, history and fraternity, to keep our Republic true to its high tradition of liberty under law.   Today, remembering the brave days of old, when men poured out their blood that their sons might be free, we give thanks to God for our country, reverently invoking His blessing upon its many races united in brotherhood, upon its unconstrained religious life, upon its passion for education, its cities shining in the sunlight, its countless homes, its pacific spirit, and its promise of a future greater than its past.

THE FOURTH OF JULY

A S Freemasons, it is in no perfunctory spirit
that we remember the 148th anniversary of
the adoption of the Declaration of American Independence, July 4th, 1776. It is a part of the history
of our country and the history of our Craft; and
it is our belief that a people who forget, or treat
lightly, a great past, cannot have a great future.
If they are indifferent to, or take as a matter of
course, what cost so much in suffering and sacrifice,
they are not worthy of the treasure they possess.

Happily, the old disputes which led up to the
American Revolution, and the legacy of enmity
which it left, are now faded and forgotten, and we
think with kindness and respect of the land against
which our forefathers fought. Since that far-off
time America and Britain have joined hands in a
vast enterprise, and their sons have fought side by
side in a world war for the liberation of mankind
and the redemption of civilization. But the American Revolution itself still stands, not only as the
birth-hour of our Republic, but as the beginning of
a new and great era in the history of humanity,
the meaning and measure of which we do not yet
see or understand.

No story outside of fairyland is more romantic
than the history of the growth and development

of our Republic.   He is a strange man, and no
patriot at all, who can read the record and not feel
his heart beat faster, stirred by a holy memory and
an honorable pride.   From thirteen thinly settled
states, united in the struggle for freedom and in
loyalty to a newly written Constitution, our nation
has grown to be one of the greatest, strongest, most
far-stretching nations on earth, a human marvel and
a social wonder.   Never has there been such a
flowing together of peoples, such a blending of
bloods, as in America.   No one race, no one influence made America: it is a fraternal achievement
in which many races and many forces mingled to
build a freer and gentler Fatherland of Mankind.

Among the creative forces by which America has
been made so great, none has been more benign
than the influence of Freemasonry.   The real history of Masonry in America belongs of right to the
genius of poetry, and its story is an epic.   Silent,
ever-present, always active, by its constructive
genius our Fraternity built itself into the very
foundations of the Republic.   When our fathers
affirmed that "governments derive their just powers from the consent of the governed," Masonry was
present assenting to one of its own principles.
What patriotic memories cluster about the old
Green Dragon Tavern in Boston!   Webster called
it "the headquarters of the Revolution," and there
was also the headquarters of Freemasonry, where
the Boston Tea Party was planned.

As in Massachusetts, so throughout the Colonies,
Masonry was everywhere active, indirectly as an
Order, but directly through its members, in behalf

of a nation "conceived in liberty and dedicated to the proposition that all men are created equal"; which is one of its basic truths. It was not an accident that so many Masons signed the Declaration of Independence, or that Washington and most of his generals were members of the Craft. Nor was it by mere chance that our first President was a Mason, sworn into office on a Bible taken from a Masonic Altar, by the Grand Master of New York. Such facts are symbols of deeper facts, showing the place and power of Masonry in the making of the nation.

Along the Atlantic coast, among the Great Lakes, in the wilderness of the Middle West, in the far South and the far West, everywhere, in centers of population and in little Upper Rooms on the frontier, the Lodge stood alongside the Home, the School, and the Church. Who can measure the influence, much less estimate the worth, of thousands of Masonic altars in this land where, all down our history, men have met in the name of God and the moral law, seeking to create that influence and sentiment which gives law its authority and touches with intellectual and spiritual refinement the life of society! Only a pen endowed with more than earthly skill could trace such an influence and tell such a story.

As Freemasons we believe that the things that made our Republic great in the past—made it not only possible, but powerful—are the things that will make it still greater in the future. A great English editor recently wrote an article asking the question, What has made America great? Not its rich resources, he said, because other lands—Russia, for example—are equally rich. Nor is it the intelligence and enterprise of our people, because others are also intelligent. No, what has made America great, he said, is its form of government. If ever of any men, it can be said that our fathers were divinely taught and divinely led when they instituted our form of government, in which individual initiative is united with social responsibility—liberty under law, liberty founded in right and reason, modified by private duty, public obligation, and a sense of the common good.

For that reason we need today, all of us, a new baptism of the spirit of citizenship, of public-mindedness, of devotion to the state for what we can put into it and not for what we can get out of it. So, and only so, can we make our form of government effective for its high ends, and vindicate the wisdom of our fathers. Today hardly half of our people who are entitled to vote ever vote on any issue. Even the excitement of a presidential campaign, such as that in which we are now engaged, does not bestir them from their lethargy. With such negligence and indifference how can the words of Lincoln be fulfilled when he declared this to be a government "of the people, by the people, for the people"? The facts show that it is not the foreign element who fail to vote, but those who are of American ancestry and training.

Here is where Masonry can render a real service, as well as in helping to create a more vivid sense of the sanctity of law. The increase of lawlessness in America in the last twenty-five years has been

appalling. Even before the Great War some kinds
of crime had increased fifteen hundred per cent.
For anyone to think lightly of our Constitution, or
any part of it, is to strike a blow at the basis of
ordered civic life. To obey only such laws as suit
our fancy or interest or appetite, is to lead the
way to anarchy. Others, by the same principle,
may disregard other laws—even those protecting
life and the ownership of property—and the result
will be chaos. Lincoln was right when he said that
obedience to law must be the political religion of
our Republic.

The growth of racial rancor among us bodes no
good for us or for our children. If left unchecked,
it will poison private fellowship and pollute public
life, injecting into the body politic germs of ills
sure to breed all sorts of social diseases. As has
been said, no one race made America; it is a fraternal adventure of many races, each adding something of precious worth to the total achievement.
Seven nationalities were represented on the May-
flower alone. By the facts of its history, no less
than by the spirit of its laws, America must know
nothing of the Saxon race, nothing of the Teutonic
race, nothing of the Slavic race. It must know only
the Human Race, of whose future and fulfillment
it is the last great hope and promise, if it is true
to its genius of liberty, toleration, and fraternity.

There is room for everything in America except
hatred. If we have been careless and sentimental
in the past about allowing so many people of different races to enter our country, we must correct
the error. But those who are already here are en-

titled to our regard, and only love, good will, and the spirit of fraternity can Americanize men and women, much less little children. Americanization is not a formula—it is a friendship. If we allow people of many races to knock at our doors, we do not want them to "knock" our institutions after we open the doors and admit them. Nor must we "knock" them. People whom we admit through the gates of America must not be foreigners, but friends. If they are often clannish, it is because we are indifferent. What we want for all is not simply freedom and opportunity, but fraternity— mutual respect and good will.

Here Masonry, by its very genius and purpose, can render a real service to the Republic, and at the same time strengthen its foundations. An instance in point is the Roosevelt Lodge in Rhode Island, almost every charter member of which was a man of a different race. The purpose of the Lodge was to bring men of many races together at the Altar of Masonry, and it was a happy thought to name the Lodge for the man who, more than any great American of recent times, exemplified in his spirit and temper the wider fraternity of races. He was the incarnation of fraternalism, and, by that token, a truly great Mason whose soul goes marching on, leading us out of bitterness toward brotherhood.

Since the Great War there has been an unhappy revival of religious intolerance in America. In nothing was the founding of our Republic more significant than in the new relation which it established between Church and State. Our fathers separated the two forever, but they gave equal liberty and honor to all elevating and benign religions. Such is also the spirit and teaching of Freemasonry, a great and simple principle which our Craft had learned and practiced before the name "United States" had ever been spoken. Toleration is not enough; we need insight, appreciation, understanding, if we are to have many races without rancor, and many faiths without fanaticism. Our religion must be a part of our patriotism, and our patriotism must be religious in its depth, warmth, and power. America is our Holy Land—sacred to our thoughts and dear to our hearts—and we dare not let it be darkened by lawlessness, defiled by racial rancor, or disfigured by religious intolerance. Narrowness of thought and littleness of spirit are out of place in the land of the large and liberal air where the future of humanity lies.

So, once more, in memory of our national birthday, all Freemasons ask all Americans, of every race, creed and condition, to renew their vows of love, honor and loyalty to our Constitution, to our President, and to our Flag which is the immortal symbol of all that is sacred in our life and law and history. Nay, more, we ask all to join hands and hearts in behalf of a greater America tomorrow, worthy of the mighty America of the past, to which, like the men who signed the Declaration of Independence, "we mutually pledge to each other our Lives, our Fortunes, and our Sacred Honor."

MASONIC EDUCATION

IN the matter of Masonic education, a bit of experience may not be amiss, and perhaps timely and worth while in view of the increasing desire on the part of the Craft to educate Masons in Masonry. It means much that we are at last awake to the need of training young Masons in the laws, customs, history, and symbols of the Order, for where there is a will there is a way, though in an undertaking so large and difficult it may take time to find the right way.

When I was made a Mason I began to ply the Master of the Lodge with questions as to what it was all about. It was a totally new thing to me, unlike anything I had ever met—a new world, with a law and language of its own, different from any environment I had known—and my curiosity stimulated my audacity. The Master did not give me much information, and much of what he gave me I learned later was wide of the mark. He knew the Ritual, but what the Ritual meant, beyond its obvious moral teaching, he did not know; nor could he tell me its history.

Instead, he referred me to a venerable Past Master, a Judge on the bench, an able and noble man, who was good enough to spend several evenings with me, talking over Masonic affairs. A man of rich culture, of gentle and charming personality, the spirit of Masonry was in his life as color is in the flower, and he gave me, both by his conversation and the impress of his character, an exalted conception of the Craft. But he did not teach me much in the way of specific information as to the origin, growth, and development of the Craft.

There, for a time, my search ended, and while I went to Lodge occasionally, and enjoyed its fellowship, to say nothing of its "big meets and big eats," I gradually drifted away. No doubt it was my fault, but I have a feeling that neither the Lodge nor the Grand Lodge did its duty by me when, as a young man and minister, I entered the Temple seeking for knowledge, and finding none. Anyway, I do not think I was entirely to blame if I became a rather rusty Mason who regarded the Fraternity as simply one more order to belong to—nothing else.

Some years later I went to Iowa, and when I tried to get into a Lodge I well-nigh failed to get in at all, though I had been asked to speak. The brother who examined me said afterward that had he not known that I was a minister, and a man of my word, he would not have allowed me to get in. Nor do I blame him, because I had forgotten about everything except the penalties of the obligations and the Grand Masonic word—and I gave that with some hesitation. Happily, by the time I became Chaplain of the Grand Lodge I had rubbed some of the rust off, and could go freely from Lodge to Lodge.

At that time a few brethren in the Grand Lodge

had begun to feel the need of Masonic education, and I became interested at once, doing a lot of work in the Grand Lodge library—the greatest in the world; and as I dug and delved, the meaning of Masonry began to unfold, in a way to startle and amaze me. The writings of Waite, with whom I had come in contact in another connection, did most for me at first, in giving me a long and large vision of the spiritual aspect of the Craft. Pike helped too, especially in a little manuscript volume of his which I found in the House of the Temple in Washington.

Out of studies such as these grew the little book called "The Builders" which, if it were written now, would be very different from what it is; more simple, more like a primer. It was written for the Grand Lodge, and has since gone into many places, showing that it was an attempt, at least, to meet a deeply felt need. As a result of my studies, and especially the reading of the reports of the Research Lodges of England, I proposed that we have a Research Lodge in Iowa, under the auspices of the Grand Lodge. From this grew the Research Society, which, fortunately, was made national in scope, and is still busy in its benign labors.

II

My experience as editor of *The Builder* taught me more than I taught the brethren; a great deal more in fact. Slowly I began to see that we had hold of a big idea, but we had it by the wrong end. To be sure, we did draw together a goodly company of brethren who were students of Masonry, as readers of and writers for *The Builder,* and that was so far good. But, in comparison with the number of Masons in America, they were very few —hardly a drop in the bucket. Indeed, we did not even touch the rank and file of the Craft, because, as I began to see, we overshot them by fifty-five miles, three hundred yards, and seventeen inches.

Then came the war, which took me away to England, and upset all my plans, one of which was to alter our policy entirely and, if possible, get hold of the other end of the idea we were working on. Books, journals, Research Societies could never do the thing that needed to be done. So much was clear—nor did I know how it could be done; but I meant to try and find out. During my first month in England I went to pay a long promised visit to Lodge Progress in Glasgow, and there met Bro. A. S. McBride, who has recently left us to join the Great White Lodge.

Never shall I forget a talk we had together in his lovely home after Lodge, which lasted until far into the night—until a sweet voice from upstairs reminded us that we had better "turn in"—a voice, alas, now silent. Knowing that my host was a great Masonic teacher, I described to him our problem and confided our difficulties. In reply he told me how he was trained in Masonry, and I thought then, as I think now, that he had the key to the whole situation, if we are wise enough to use it. In the old days in Scotland, he said, it was the custom—now, unfortunately, fallen into disuse—to have what they called "intenders," that is brethren whose special duty it was to post young men in the Ritual, but also, at the same time, to instruct them in the things they ought to know about the Craft and its work in the world.

There it is, beyond doubt, the plan and method we need. It takes a young man at the time when he is ready and eager to know; it links the study of Masonry with the Ritual, as it should be; and it is done in an atmosphere in which not only the facts, but the spirit, the "feel" of Masonry, can be communicated. There is not a Lodge in the land in which there are not a number of brethren capable, or who can become capable, of such instruction. Surely a Grand Lodge ought to be as eager to have at least an elementary knowledge of what Masonry is imparted to its young men, as it is to have them know the Ritual. Had there been such an "intender" in my Lodge when I was made a Mason, he would have been a godsend—just the man I wanted to meet.

Such a plan is neither impossible nor impractical, if we really mean business in the matter of Masonic education. Where is a young man to go if not to his Lodge and his Grand Lodge in order to learn what Masonry is? Why should he have to go anywhere else? If it is said that he can read if he wishes to learn, what is he to read? More than half the books written about Masonry are rubbish and rot, written by men ill-trained or half-baked, who foist every kind of odd and curious notion upon their unsuspecting readers in the name of Masonry. Surely there is enough authentic fact and truth about Masonry to form a body of knowledge to be taught to young Masons. If not, we are in a poor way indeed, and it is time to ease up on our high-sounding talk about the antiquity and profundity of our symbols, to say nothing of the peroration we know so well.

Such is the situation as I have come to see it, after some experience and not a little observation and reflection. Whether my glasses are clear or smoked, I leave it for the brethren to decide. But surely it is high time for our Grand Lodges, either separately or together, as they think best, to take up the problem of giving some kind of training to our rapidly growing Craft, that our young men may know what Masonry is, what it means, and what to do with it. Anyway, I should like to do something to make it easier for a young man to learn more what he ought and has a right to know about Masonry than I found it in my day.

III

In regard to the working of the plan here proposed, let me add a few details of a practical sort. Here, again, I speak from actual experience. Often each season I am asked to visit Lodges, and nearly always it is to give a talk following the degree, in place of the "historical" lecture. The men want something different from the lecture in the Ritual, which has become a mere rigmarole. My talk is usually a brief, bird's-eye sketch of the origin and growth of the Craft, how it came to be and what it is trying to do in the world—a simple story made up of facts about which there is little or no debate.

The expressions of interest and the questions asked afterward, show that for most of the brethren the story is entirely new. A sketch of the Men's House in early society, of the drama of the Ancient Mysteries upon which our great degree is modeled, what the great symbols meant to men in early times, when and why Masons were called *Free*masons, how far back men who were not actual working Masons asked to be *Accepted* as members in the Lodges, the story of the first Grand Lodge, and such like facts are novel and interesting. Hundreds of brethren—young men, especially—have told me that my simple talk made them feel that Masonry had a real meaning and a history, and is not a thing in the air—like a fairy-story.

What I do in a simple talk ought to be done by the Lodge itself, under the authority and direction, of course, of the Grand Lodge. Suppose a Grand Lodge should decide to teach Masonry to its young men, how would it go about such an undertaking? The first thing would be to select a group of Masonic scholars to prepare a digest of the facts to be taught as to the origin and development of the Craft. This material should then be carefully worked over and arranged, say, in three historical lectures, in the manner of a Ritual—simple, clear, accurate—approved by the Grand Lodge. So much knowledge ought to be required of every man who is elected to the Chair of a Lodge, if only to do away with the absurdity of a man being the Master of a Lodge who knows nothing about Masonry.

If some such requirement were made necessary to

Mastership, in a few years the whole problem of "intenders," to use the old Scotch phrase, would be solved. Every Past Master, as well as the men in line for the Chair, would be qualified to instruct an initiate not only in the Ritual, but in the story, symbols, laws and customs of the Craft. Each initiate would then know the primary facts of Masonic history and tradition, and would be free to follow further and learn more as his inclination and opportunity might direct. At any rate, he would have the basis and beginning—the grade-school foundation, so to name it—of a Masonic education; and we may be sure that few would stop there.

What should be taught to Masons in the Lodge? Besides the outline of the history and evolution of the Craft which I have suggested, each Mason ought to know the story of his own Lodge and of his Grand Lodge. It was years before I had the faintest idea of the history of the Grand Lodge of Iowa, under whose obedience I live. Yet what a story it is, interwoven with the story of the Commonwealth—a romance of the pioneers, of brave beginnings when the State was a Territory and the Lodge was busy as a creative and beneficient influence in formative days. What is true of Iowa is true of every State in the Union. Who can read the Masonic history of Texas, for example—or Michigan, or Ohio, or Kansas, to say nothing of the longer history of the older states—and not feel his heart grow warm with pride and reverence?

There is not a Grand Lodge in America whose story is not a thrilling romance, and it ought to be known by the young men who live under its obedience. The right kind of lecture—or more than one—prepared with care, giving the facts and their human color and social setting—given in every Lodge in the jurisdiction once or twice or quarterly each year, would mean a new generation of Masons proud of their Masonry and ready to carry forward the great tradition into the years that lie ahead. How little we have done, how much remains to be done!

ST. JOHN'S DAY

I

OF the Masonic feasts of St. John the Baptist and St. John the Evangelist much has been written, but to little account. The two feasts, coming at the time of the summer and winter solstices, are of course older than Christianity, being reminiscences of the old Light Religion, in which Masonry had its origin.

In pre-Christian times the Roman Collegia were wont to adopt pagan deities as patrons. When Christianity came, the names of its saints—some of them martyrs of the Order of the Builders— were substituted for the old pagan gods. Just why, when, and by whom the two Saints John were chosen as the patron saints of Masonry—instead of St. Thomas, who is the patron saint of Architecture —has never been made clear.

Legend has been busy trying to explain, but we cannot be sure of what it tells us. Also many reasons have been given, but they are reasons after the fact. The Gospel of St. John is the most Masonic of the Gospels, if only because its central theme is Light. It portrays Jesus as the Light of the World, and His Gospel as the Gospel of Light. Lodges were dedicated to "the Holy Saint John" and Masons were called "John's Brothers," no doubt for the reason that Masonry is a quest after Light.

An old legend tells us that after the destruction of Jerusalem, A.D. 70, the Order, then in decline, besought St. John then living in Ephesus, and over ninety years of age, to become its Grand Master, and that he did so, saying that he had been initiated into the Craft as a young man. It is only a legend, to be sure, but the Old Charges speak of St. John the Evangelist as a Saint of the Craft. St. John the Baptist seems to have come into the Craft after the Reformation, and it was on his day, in 1717, that the Grand Lodge of England was organized "according to ancient usage."

Whatever the facts may be, surely it is in accordance with the fitness of things that we honor these two names, John the Baptist, the stern prophet of righteousness, and John the Evangelist, the teacher of Love. Righteousness and Love—those two words do not fall short of telling the whole duty of a man and a Mason.

II

Thinking of St. John's Day, one remembers the extraordinary drama entitled *John the Baptist,* by Hermann Sudermann, showing how the sun-burned desert prophet, preaching of impending wrath, was softened and won by the new and strange Gospel of Love. While it reveals John as the central figure, it is at the same time a Christ-drama of amazing beauty and power.

Stern, stately, and magnificent is the Baptist, as
we see him in the desert, surrounded by the multi-
tude. His words flash fire as he lays the ax at the
root of the evils of the day, denouncing the sins
of the people, and foretelling the coming of a greater
than he. "He shall come—He must," cries the
Voice in the Wilderness. It is a vivid picture as
the artist sees it, with the play of oriental color over
its mingled passions of love, hate, revenge and mob-
fury.

For news comes that Herod, who has taken
Herodias to wife, is preparing to lead her in procession into the Temple. Stung by the outrage
upon religion, John hurries to Jerusalem. The
scene shifts and we see the desert seer enter the
Holy City, not unlike the triumphal entry of Jesus
later, welcomed by the people and the leader of a
protest against Herod, if not against Rome.

In the court of the Temple, by chance, John en-
counters Amasai, a skilled Pharisee, who engages
him in debate about a point of law. Unused to
such entanglements, John is plainly confused, until
he bursts out in wrath and affirms that he has no
fault to find with the law, but with its administra-
tion. A group of Galilean pilgrims are attracted
by the dispute, and one of them, an old woman,
brushes against Amasai, who draws his robe close
about him, lest he, a chosen Pharisee, be made impure by her touch.

Simon, a Galilean, tells the woman not to touch
the Pharisee, lest she be contaminated. When
asked by what right he used such words, he said,
"Higher than law or sacrifice is Love." John turns

to Simon, drawn by the new word Love, and asks where he had heard it, adding: "It is so simple, yet so fearful."

Confusion follows, and both Simon and the Pharisee vanish. Upon entering the city John had gone to the palace and rebuked Herod to his face. Herodias coolly asks him if he, who lives in the desert, knows the lives of men. She says:

"You seem to me to be so distant that the very beat of the human heart appears to you to be folly. The hot wind has taught you to hate—but what do you know of those who live and die for the sake of love?"

"You speak of love—even you!" cries John, who none the less felt the point of her thrust. "Do you know in what forms sin likes best to appear? Say Pride, say Hate, say what you will, and I will laugh at you. Sin likes best to call itself Love."

So speaking, he turns away, an intense struggle going on in him between his hatred and the new teaching about love. Herod goes, with Herodias, to enter the Temple, and John picks up a stone to throw at him. Urged by the crowd to throw it, he raises his arm—and then, hardly knowing what he is doing, slowly lets the stone fall out of his hand to the ground, "In the name of Him who made me love you."

That night John sends two of his disciples to Jesus to learn the new truth. As they go he takes them by the hand and says: "It seems to me that I love you." When they are gone, he goes to find Simon of Galilee, and fails. However, he meets two Galilean merchants, who tell him about Jesus, in whom they have evidently taken only a passing interest. But they recall some of His words:

"Love your enemies and bless them that curse you. Resist not evil. Pray for them that despitefully use you. If a man smite you on one cheek, turn to him the other also."

At hearing these words, carelessly reported as absurdities, John stands as one transfixed, trying to think them through, "It is so simple, yet so fearful," he keeps saying, as if trying to lay hold of an elusive and inscrutable force, too fine to capture, yet too mighty to resist. Morning finds him with his great head bowed upon his breast, deeply agitated and distraught.

Still deep in thought, he is arrested, taken before Herod, where he sees Salome dance, and hears her ask for his head as a reward. Herod pronounces sentence, but grants respite until John can hear from Jesus. In the last scene the two disciples return and report. They tell of the gentleness of Jesus, the light in His face, the joy-giving power of His smile; and then His message to John, which closes with the words: "Blessed is he who is not filled with anger against me."

A new and tender light shines in the soul of John. He sees now why his lips are sealed, and why his power must decrease—that he who would judge, must know love. At the end John the Prophet prophesies of "The Kingdom of peace and the Prince of Peace, whose sword is Love and whose battle cry is mercy. The bridegroom cometh, and my joy is fulfilled."

Such a poor sketch gives no inkling of the richness and beauty of the drama of love melting wrath by its own inner power. "It is so simple, yet so fearful," is the sum of it all. It is an exquisite interpretation of "that strange power which men call weakness," of which St. John the Evangelist was a preacher.

THE PRACTICE OF TOLERA-
TION

SINCE the Great War, all over the world, the spirit of intolerance has returned to torment our race. It takes many forms, both religious and political, as if, for the time at least, the rule of Reason had given way to the rule of Force. Such a mood usually follows in the wake of war, due to the fear and anger which war leaves in the hearts of men. So vast was the upheaval, so deeply did it stir the primitive passions, that we cannot expect it all at once to subside.

It is surely remarkable, and not a little depressing, that in America, among a people and under a government where freedom of thought, freedom of speech, freedom of worship are embedded in the rock of our basic law, there should be such an outbreak of intolerance. One would think such a thing impossible, if the people had any clear idea of the teaching of our history or the spirit of our ideals. Yet there are communities in our country which are almost armed camps, threatened with war about different religious beliefs. The rights of minorities are ignored, and the arm of the law is actually used to compel obedience not only to the moral teachings of religion, but also to enforce its dogmas—a fact so startling that it stuns us.

Here is an opportunity for Masonry—itself once the victim of a terrible intolerance in America, a hundred years ago this very year—to present to this nation a noble exhibit of those ideals which have been the glory of its history. The spirit which mars our American life today will eventually destroy its best traits unless Masons, and others of like mind, exert every influence within their power to halt it, and bring the nation back to a better mood and a truer method. The ideals we cherish at the Altar must be taught publicly and urged upon our people, in behalf of the widest possible relations with our fellow man and a more appreciative understanding and goodwill.

Long ago Dr. Johnson, in his Dictionary, said that toleration, though a good word, was not much used. Today we might add that while toleration is still a good word it is not practiced as it should be, even by those who use it. Not a little of the friction of our time is the result of men trying to impose their ideas and codes upon others, not by reason and persuasion, but by force of numbers or some kind of pressure. Men cannot long live together in an orderly society without toleration, and there can be no real toleration other than the outgrowth of the spirit of tolerance—the spirit of live and let live, think and let think, whereby we agree to disagree and yet retain respect and the courtesies of life.

Clear thinking and right feeling are both needed, if we are to be really tolerant; and we must know what we mean by the words we use. Tolerance is a spirit in the hearts of men; toleration is the way

in which that spirit manifests itself. It is the mark
of a well-balanced mind and temper, sure of itself
and equally sure of what it holds to be true. Toleration does not mean indifference to truth or
weakness in defending it. The indifferent man is
not tolerant; he is merely indulgent. What Emerson called "a mush of concessions" is not toleration;
it is just mushiness. Much of what passes for
toleration in our time is simply lazy, hazy indifference, an open-mindedness so open that ideas go in
one ear and out the other. A man who lets error
be as good as truth, or to whom one idea is as good
as another, is not tolerant; he is dead of mind.

No, toleration is not indifference. It is not neu-
trality, a refusal to take sides. Nor is it approval
of error. It is not negative, but positive. Only a
man who has clear and firm beliefs can be tolerant
in any true meaning of the word. But he has such
faith in his faith that he will not try to force it
upon others, save in the only spirit, and by the
only method, by which faith ought to win its way.
He will stand for his faith, he will fight for it, but
he will use reason and not force, persuasion and
not punishment, in seeking to bring men to his own
way of thinking. In short, a tolerant man is one
who, realizing the dignity of truth and the worth
of the human mind, grants to every man the right
which he claims for himself, to shape his own ideas
and beliefs in his own way, to advocate them, and
make them prevail if he can.

Put in another way, toleration is the middle way
between the falsehood of extremes, a balance between bigotry and indifference. It rests not upon

uncertainty, as some hold, but upon certitude—a sense of the reality and power of truth, and the assurance that if he is loyal to the truth it will win over what he holds to be error. It is *intolerance* that rests upon uncertainty and fear. At bottom every bigot is a sceptic, afraid that if he does not drive his idea into the minds of men it cannot win its way. Always it is the narrow idea that is bigoted, and the narrow man who is intolerant— the man who imagines that he has all truth shut up within his creed or dogma. By the same fact, as a wise teacher has pointed out, the responsibility for toleration rests upon the man of wider vision and deeper faith.

Toleration, then, is love of truth united with love of man. Love of truth alone may lead to every kind of cruelty—it will crucify its fellow man upon a cross of creed. Love of man alone ends in sentimentalism. Only when the two are joined do we have true toleration, as when Jesus rebuked His disciples for wanting to bring down fire from heaven to burn up men who were doing the same good work in another way. Toleration is the willing consent to disagreement, a sense of the sanctity of difference, the desire to see other points of view, and the earnest effort to win others, by reason and love, to the vision of truth as we see it. Hence the wisdom of the Book of Holy Law when it tells us to "speak the truth in love," because, if we are to win men to the truth it must be as much by friendship as by philosophy, by goodwill no less than by good logic.

No doubt there would be wide differences of

faith and opinion if everybody understood and
loved everybody else, because human minds are
different and see things in different ways; but we
do not realize how far the scattered mists of mis-
understanding, which gather into great clouds of
controversy, and make for bitterness and bigotry
among men, are due to a mistranslation of motives
and ideas—lack of sympathy, fellowship, and goodwill between man and man.

At the same time we ought to draw a clear line
between an ignoble and a noble toleration. Indifference, as has been said, is not toleration at all. Or
a man who is forced to be tolerant because it is
prudent for him to be so is not truly tolerant; the
spirit is not in his heart. Or, again, the man who
is tolerant because he cannot help himself may turn
out to be intolerant if he has the power. The man
who is really tolerant is the man who has the power
to be intolerant if he would, but refuses to do so. He
has such respect for the spirit of man, such sympathy for the limitations of his fellow men and
their struggle for the truth, and above all, such a
sense of the vastness of Truth that it is an article
of his faith that all men should be free to seek the
truth and to serve such truth as they find.

Oddly enough, so far there has been no great
book tracing the growth of the spirit of toleration
in the heart of the race. The story of Intolerance
has been told, and it is a history so horrible that
it makes the blood run cold. What blind bigotry,
what hideous tortures, what unbelievable brutality
and refinements of cruelty—much of it in the name
of religion! If half the time and power spent in

killing men for their faith had been devoted tc
education and friendship, the earth would have
been a Garden of Eden long ago. To what heights
of knowledge and wisdom the human mind would
have soared! If the principle of Toleration had
been practiced, or if those had done so who pro-
fessed the faith of Christ, to what degree of happiness and progress the race would have climbed!

Yet, if history makes any fact plain it is that
intolerance is a failure, as well as a folly. It failed
in its effort to destroy the early Christian Church
—forgetting that the blood of martyrs is the seed
of truth. It failed with the Scottish Covenanters,
who were hunted and hounded to death for their
faith, since only a coward will let his faith and
worship be dictated by others. It failed when
Roger Williams was driven into winter snow to
found a free society in the wilderness. It failed
when they cut off the head of King Charles and
made a martyr out of a fool. Reaction followed,
and a riot of immortality and scepticism, as one
extreme always follows another.

Against so dark a background the history of the
growth of the spirit of toleration reads like a romance. It is the noblest tradition of the race. The
brave men who dared, at the risk of life and fortune,
to fight for the freedom of faith and the rights of
the mind to seek the truth, deserve the eternal
gratitude of humanity. Their names shine like
stars in the crown of the world. The soldier who
faces a machine gun is not more heroic than were
the men who faced prison, the thumb-screw, and
the burning stake for the right to worship God in

the way their hearts loved best. Every man, every Mason especially, ought to read the six great books on Toleration—they stand like milestones along the way to liberty, and mark the journey of man toward the light.

In America, of all lands, men ought to be tolerant, if only because our freedom of faith has cost so much and means so much. It was in quest of religious freedom that men sought the shores of the New World, to escape the bigotry of Church and State alike. Yet as a fact, which few remember, much less realize, up until the Revolution and for years afterward, Church and State were united in America. The long fight, led by Jefferson, in behalf of a free Church in a free country, is one of the most gallant chapters in our history. It was not until 1779 that the chains were broken, setting both Church and State free. The plea of Jefferson in behalf of Tolerance is one of the noblest documents in our annals; it ought to be read in our lodges and recited in our schools. It is a part of our sacred writings.

Long before Jefferson made his great plea— twenty years before he was born—Freemasonry had made a pronouncement so prophetic that it reads like a Divine revelation. If written yesterday it would be remarkable, but when we remember that the article on "God and Religion" in the Constitutions was set forth in 1723, amidst sectarian rancor and intolerance unimaginable, it stands out as a mountain peak in the history of freedom and fraternity. He is a strange Mason who can read that old document, so little known to the world at large, and not feel his heart beat high with pride and warm with an obligation to be a tolerant man, free from bigotry, and a seeker after "the means of conciliating true friendship among persons that might have remained at a perpetual distance."

It is because men are kept at a "perpetual distance" that they are intolerant; they do not know one another. When they meet in mutual respect and good will, as they do in the lodge, and lay their minds side by side, they discover that there is a "religion in which all men agree," and that it is more profound and important than surface differences. The secret of Masonry, almost too simple to be found out, is that it asks men to accept the facts of religion—faith in God, the reality of the moral law, and the hope of life after death—as the basis of fellowship, and allow each man to interpret and expound those facts in his own way. So it has achieved unity without uniformity, and a fellowship in which freedom and fraternity are joined.

From the founding of the first modern Grand Lodge in 1717 down to our own time, in every oath, lesson, lecture and symbol of every rite and rank, Masonry has been a teacher of toleration—its lodges oases of good will in a world of feud. The Great Schism in the Mother Grand Lodge, from 1752 to 1831, had to do largely with the religious issue, but it was finally settled not by a contraction but by an expansion of the principle of toleration —an enlargement of fellowship to include the men of other religions, and allowing them to take their oath of obligation upon the sacred books of their own faith. In all this Masonry has been a pioneer.

leading men into a larger fellowship, and if it is true to its genius and history, it will finally lead men beyond toleration into a unity of those who love in the service of those who need.

Toleration, as Albert Pike told us in golden words, is not enough; it is a truce, not a peace. Merely to endure, to bear with a man whose belief is unlike our own, implies the right to dictate if we would; and we have no such right. Also, it implies that we are infallibly right, and that is sheer vanity. The spirit of Masonry, like its great and simple faith, goes beyond mere toleration. It seeks sympathy, understanding, and co-operation in behalf of the making of better men and the building of a better world. For that reason it opens wide its portals and invites men to enter and learn how to live the Brotherly Life in an unbrotherly world.

Because this is so, because Masonry, by all the obligations of its history and its teaching, no less than by the promptings of its spirit, is a Temple of Toleration, a special responsibility is laid upon it in a day of faction and feud. In a day when Churches are rent with schism, and sect is divided against sect, race against race, and class against class, the world needs men of wider vision and kinder hearts—"large, eternal fellows"—tall enough to see over walls of creed and form and party, and plan and work for the common good. Never has there been a greater opportunity for Masonry than today, and if it fails the failure will be tragic beyond belief or hope of repair.

The future of the race lies in the keeping of three mighty and benign forces: the Spirit of Science, the

Democratic Principle, and a practical Fraternal Religion. Without free and honest inquiry we cannot find the truth, and once it is found it must belong to all and be used for the good of all, without regard to class or race, to relieve the cruelty and suffering of mankind. To use the skill of science for the good of all asks for a fraternal religion, for it is only under the impulse of spiritual ideals that the common good can be realized. What a world we could make if men took for their motto: *"We are agreed to disagree; we are resolved to love; we are united to serve."*

Or, to put it in Masonic terms, which mean more the more one ponders their depth and meaning; Brotherly Love, Relief, and Truth—that is, Truth used in the spirit of Brotherly Love for the Relief of mankind from ignorance, injustice, and inhumanity. Men are selfish and mean and bigoted and brutal because they do not know the truth. War follows because we have not learned to live together by the laws of fraternity. Much of our life is a jungle of snapping envy and gouging greed because we have not found out the plain fact that each man, each race, can find the highest good only in the common good.

> Whether the time be slow or fast
>   Enemies, hand in hand,
> Must come together at the last
>   And understand.
>
> No matter how the die is cast,
>   Or who may seem to win—

We know that we must love at last—
Why not begin?

To that high and holy end, though it be a "far-off Divine event," let us dedicate ourselves anew, taking vows each in his heart and together at the Altar of the Lodge, to make the Masonry of the future, like the Masonry of the past, a Temple of Reverence and Toleration—using the word reverence in the threefold way in which Goethe, a Mason, taught us to use it: Reverence for God, for man, for all life and duty. What though a narrow bigotry may belie and a rancorous hate misunderstand, we know a secret, the greatest ever learned by man, never better told than by a master poet who is a Master Mason:

He drew a circle that shut me out,
Heretic, rebel, a thing to flout;
But love and I had the wit to win,
We drew a circle that took him in.

EDWIN BOOTH AS A MASON

IN Gramercy Park, New York, in front of the Players Club, stands the slender, graceful figure of Edwin Booth, fixed in the eternal repose of art. Designed by Quinn—who also wrought the bust of Poe in Poe Park—it reveals the vanished actor in his favorite rôle of Hamlet, which temperament, training, and personality had made peculiarly his own. How few know that the master of tragedy was also a Master Mason, and that his one great ambition was to be a Master of a Lodge. He was nowhere more at ease than in a Lodge, and nowhere more welcome. Hence a little research among his relatives and friends, the results of which are offered herewith, along with certain observations on a man who was as noble in his life as he was great in his art.

Those who wish to know the story of Booth in detail—and a memorable story it is, worthy of being told many times—may find it recorded with exquisite insight and skill in the "Life and Art of Edwin Booth," by William Winter, the Plutarch of our stage. Truly, it is a fascinating book, as much for its descriptions of Booth on the stage as for its account of his habits in private life—for, in the art of interpreting the personality of an artist, there is no one like Winter, no one near him. Such genius

is rare, and the more precious for that the art of
a great actor dies with him, save as it may live,
for a brief time, in the minds of the generation before whom he appears. Happily, an intimate fellowship united with literary power to preserve the
image and art of Booth, and to these was added
life-long love of the man—as witness these words:

"Farewell; nor mist, nor flying cloud,
    Nor night can ever dim
The wreath of honors pure and proud,
    Our hearts have twined for him!"

Spiritual personality eludes definition; to be is
more than to do, and the soul of Edwin Booth was
greater even than his achievements. He was a
benefactor to thousands, revealing to them, now
in forms of beauty and color, now in shapes of
terror and power, the wonder of human nature and
its destiny. By birth and heredity he possessed
those qualities of beauty, grace, charm, and expression which others strive in vain to attain. His
face, his voice, his gesture, and his brilliant and
beautiful spirit gave him conquest—those dark
eyes flashing divine fire, not alone of physical vi-
tality, but of imagination, emotion, and exaltation
of soul. He had no need of novelties; he was himself a novelty. In Richelieu, Othello, Iago, Lear,
Bertuccio, and Brutus, but most of all in Hamlet,
his power was made manifest; power of insight, of
intense emotion, of richness and color of personality,
of thoughtful, brooding habit of a stately mind—
all abstracted from passion and suffused with a

mysterious melancholy and the pensive, dream-like soul of a poet. Such qualities made his Hamlet an unforgettable picture of sorrowful grandeur, sad majesty, ineffable mournfulness, and grief-stricken isolation, as of one who walked a troubled way amid the foul crimes of the living and the phantoms of the dead. Whether in the glittering halls of Elsinore, on its midnight battlements, or in its lonely, wind-beaten place of graves, the lovely, suffering, awe-struck spirit of the Prince seemed to wear once more his robe of flesh.

In private life Booth was the soul of honor, gentle, affable, often playful, and uncommonly apt in telling comic stories, albeit men felt that he dwelt somewhat apart and aloof—sometimes mistaking an excess of modesty for haughtiness whereas beneath his reserve there was an abundance of everything that could solace the declining years of an aged mother, provident of blessings, tireless in service; and his reverence for the memory of his father was akin to religion. A devout Christian in faith, he had, nevertheless, a foreboding nature, and expected every kind of disaster—except the most terrible one of all which befell him when his brother murdered Lincoln. It was pitiful to see him then, bowed low under the shadow of a tragedy greater than he had portrayed on the stage. Youth goes; age comes; and Booth passed into the sere and yellow leaf with dignity and sweetness, and never knew "the set gray life and its apathetic end."

Of his Masonic fellowship, his brother-in-law, J. H. Magonigle, writes:

Yes, Edwin Booth was an ardent Mason, and for twenty-five years before his death, on June 7, 1893, was a member of New York Lodge No. 330. He was always proud of the Fraternity, but the exactions of his profession prevented his regular attendance at Lodge. For the same reason, he was kept from being the Master of a Lodge of Masons, which was one of his dearest ambitions. Nevertheless, the Brethren held him in high esteem and were proud of his association.

Brother A. A. Auchmoedy gives this interesting reminiscence:

I was Master of a Masonic Lodge in Omaha a good many years ago. Edwin Booth was playing in the city. I knew that he was a Mason, and sent a committee over to invite him to meet with us after the play. He sent back word that he would do so with pleasure, and we sent a committee to escort him to the Lodge. The examination was brief, but entirely satisfactory, and when he entered the room every member was on his feet, greeting him with hearty applause. He seemed much interested in the closing exercises, and at the banquet which followed he was a happy member of the party. There were songs, in which Booth joined heartily with his wondrously sweet voice, and several brief speeches before the great actor was called upon. He began by saying:

"Mr. Toastmaster and Brothers: I am like a boy out of school tonight. It is a delight to be with you. If I act like a boy, kindly overlook it." Then he told many interesting stories of his connection with Masonry and of his career as an actor—how deeply grateful he had been at the forethought and tender consideration of his Brethren in times of great distress, hinting at the days when he felt himself under a cloud, when President Lincoln met his death at the hands of his brother. Continuing, he said: "I shall never forget that wherever I went Masons rallied about me and cheered my drooping spirits. But for their love and forethought I can tell you now, my brethren, I do not think I should have resumed my life as an actor after that awful event."

Suddenly he switched to a pleasantry, and had all of us laughing. His readings seemed brighter and better than they ever were on the stage. One Brother asked him what was his favorite poem, and after thinking a moment he answered: "Please put the question differently, and ask me what my favorite hymn is." We all wondered what it would be. Then, in a voice low and sweet, he said, "That hymn which the world knows as Jesus Lover of My Soul"—and without waiting he recited it as we had never heard it recited before. A member asked for his favorite piece of prose: "I thank you, my Brother," he said, "for asking that question. The most beautiful, impressive, noble, and unforgettable and uplifting words that were ever uttered and preserved to the world I shall do myself the honor of reciting. Please be standing with me." And with bowed head he recited the Lord's prayer.

Naturally, it was the dramatic element in Masonry that attracted the attention of a man like Booth, and he never ceased to wonder at the simplicity, power, and firm grip on the bitter, old and dark reality of life displayed in the drama of the Third Degree. Surely he was no mean judge of tragedy, and he left this testimony:

In all my research and study, in all my close analysis of the masterpieces of Shakespeare, in my earnest determination to make those plays appear real on the mimic stage, I have never and nowhere, met tragedy so real, so sublime, so magnificent as the legend of Hiram. It is substance without shadow—the manifest destiny of life which requires no picture and scarcely a word to make a lasting impression upon all who can understand. To be a Worshipful Master, and to throw my whole soul into that work, with the candidate for my audience and the Lodge for my stage, would be a greater personal distinction than to receive the plaudits of the people in the theatres of the world.

Toward the end, Booth lived much alone—reading, musing, pondering upon his art, and especially thinking of that one other subject which engaged him most deeply—Religion. He had the constant spirit of a believer, the impartiality of a philosopher, and the soul of a poet; and so diffused an influence of strength, grace and peace. The charm of his nature was blended composure, gentleness and power. Upon the marge of that vast mystery which encircles our little lives like a sea, he stood in awe, wonder, and confidence—and so drifted away. Around his name is a halo of romance that will never fade. His character and conduct are summed up in the words of Hamlet to Horatio, which he once wished might be his epitaph:

Thou hast been
As one, in suffering all, that suffers nothing,
A man that Fortune's buffets and rewards
Hast taken with equal thanks.

THE FUTURE OF MASONRY

E VEN a brief glimpse of the history of Modern
Masonry, its almost accidental origin and its
amazing evolution, gives one many problems to
ponder. It is an astonishing story, fit for romance,
and no man can read it without wonder. But in
our days the minds of thoughtful men turn to the
future more than to the past, thinking of the times
ahead, and they naturally ask: What part, if any,
is Masonry to have in helping to shape a better
world order?

The past is secure. Masonry had a silent but
mighty part in the making of America and in
fashioning its fundamental life and law. The story
of the American Revolution might have been very
different, had not Washington and his generals—
most of them, at any rate—been held together by
the peculiar tie which Masons spin and weave between men. But what of the future of Masonry
in America and in the world? Obviously such an
Order lies under special obligations to our country
in these tangled times. The closing paragraph of
the article on Masonry in the ninth edition of the
Encyclopædia Britannica is very significant; doubly
so because the writer was not a Mason:

"As regards the future of Freemasonry, it is impossible, at least for an outsider, to say much. The celebration of the brotherhood of man, and the cultivation of universal goodwill in the abstract, seem rather indefinite objects for any society in this unimaginative age. There is, on the other hand, a tendency to degenerate into mere conviviality; while, if schools, or asylums, or other charities are supported, to that extent of course the society becomes local and exclusive in its character. In the meantime, Masonry is to blame for keeping afloat in the minds of its members many of the most absolutely puerile ideas. A more accurate knowledge of its singular and not undignified history would tend more than anything else to give worth and elevation to its aims."

Thus even an outsider sees clearly enough that Masonry, as now organized and employed, is not adequate to the demands of a realistic generation, and that to go on making men Masons, as we are now doing by wholesale, without giving them an intelligent and authentic knowledge of what Masonry is, or what it means, with no definite objects beyond fellowship and philanthropy—objects to which other Orders are equally devoted—is for Masonry to lose, by ignorance or neglect, what has been distinctive in its history and genius, and invite degeneration, if not disaster. Indeed, not a little of the tendency in our time to turn Masonry aside from its historic spirit and purpose—to say nothing of the multiplication of extraneous, imitative, or associated orders, fanciful in purpose and fantastic in program—is due to lack of knowledge of the history of Masonry and the reason why it has held so tenaciously to certain principles and policies through so many years of storm and strife. The future of Masonry, if it is to have a future worthy of its past, will be determined by its historic genius and purpose, not in slavish adherence to details, but by loyal and constructive obedience to its peculiar spirit and tenets. Otherwise our Lodges will become mere Clubs, like a thousand other such organizations—useful and delightful in their degree, but in nowise distinctive—far removed from the original meaning and intent of the Craft.

Hence the desire and endeavor of our time, as indicated in the threefold purpose of the Masonic Service Association of the United States, that Speculative Masonry shall once more be Operative by becoming Co-operative in its spirit and labor. There is manifest in the growing mind of the Fraternity today a wider realization and a larger application of the time-honored and beautiful mission of Masonry, as expressed in its oft-declared trinity of purpose; Brotherly Love, Relief, and Truth. Let us take Relief first, since it is so fundamental that nothing need be said beyond the famous word of an eastern seer: "When man will not help man the end of the world has come." By Relief we mean the urgent necessities of humanity in time of woe, whether it be war, pestilence, or other disaster— flood, fire, earthquake—which may any day devastate any part of the world, helping not only our Brethren in dire plight, but also, to the measure of our power, all who by affliction are made helpless. An unknown poet puts it vividly, as poets know how to do:

Men in the street and mart,
Felt the same kinship of the human heart
That makes them, in face of flame and flood,
Rise to the meaning of true Brotherhood.

By truth we mean, in this connection, three
vitally important things in the service of which the
modern Masonic Craft is enlisted and devoted.
First, let it always be remembered that Freemasonry, today as in the past, by virtue alike of
its principles and history, stands for those "great
freedoms of the mind" by which men arrive at the
Truth. Our Craft is utterly committed to the principle of freedom of thought—unhampered by political and ecclesiastical dictation—the right, and also
the duty, of man to seek everywhere and in every
way for the Truth by which no man is injured, but
by which we have the only basis for freedom and
faith. Second, we mean by Truth our devotion to
the everlasting enterprise of public education without which democratic societies cannot permanently
endure. We insist upon letting in the light, letting
all the light all the way in, driving ignorance, superstition, and despotism off the earth. By the same
token, we mean that public education shall be kept
clear of sectarian influence, and clean of party or
class propaganda.

Which brings me to the matter of most importance, and that is what is to be the future of
Freemasonry, if any, in the field of public service
and world comity? Without advocating any inno-
vation in the Body of Masonry—none is needed
much less desired—it must be plain enough that

something else, something more, is needed to meet the demands of our rapidly growing Fraternity, as well as the needs of the society in which we labor, and that is an adaptation of our methods to the spirit and needs of modern life. Masonry need not change either its spirit or its principles—God forbid —but its Lodges must become increasingly, as they were in the early days of America, civic and social centers, leaders in whatever requires to be done for the common good in their communities, if they are to train, direct and utilize for the highest ends the teeming life and abounding energies of the Craft, which otherwise, as is now too much the tendency, may find vent in other and less desirable ways. Just as the Churches within the last two decades, without changing their faith or principles, have adapted, and are still adapting, their method of work and appeal to the new sense of social and community life which is so marked a feature of our generation; so Masonry must somehow find its place and take its part, or be left behind as useless—just an order to belong to, nothing more.

Masonry, as some one said, has so far been a fraternal order founded upon a philosophy of individualism, but it cannot remain so and be of much use to the modern world. Individualism, of course, is fundamental, and the work of training men in personal moral excellence is indispensable; but noble private-mindedness must become public-mindedness, with a sense of social duty and service. While Masonry rightly abjures political and sectarian disputes in its Lodges, it cannot be inactive in that vast area of opportunity, with which sectarian and partisan feuds have nothing to do, where the most important work of the world is done. Indeed, it can help to keep political trickery and dickering out of fields where they have neither right nor value, as it is now doing in defense of the American Public School, to which it has pledged allegiance.

What will America be like fifty or a hundred years hence? Even today we find ourselves in a new and almost terrifying America, where wild forces are at play and strange influences are at work. For years we have been inundated by tides of immigration, not only from lands friendly to our institutions, but from lands where our ideals are like an unknown tongue. Those multitudes will be changed by America, no doubt—by the alchemy of its large and liberal fellowship—but America, in turn, may be changed by them, unless we have a care, into something very different from what our fathers meant it to be. These and like questions are much in the minds of thoughtful men, whether Masons or not, often with alarm, sometimes with dismay, as they watch the procession of events. Surely there is abundant room for the right kind of propaganda, sanely, wisely, and intelligently American, and here Masonry may find, and is finding, a great opportunity.

Further afield, on the high and animated scene of world affairs, much is taking place the final issue of which no one can foresee. The old balance of power among nations may easily give way to a new alignment of races and colors, with consequences one dare not contemplate and possibilities that make the heart stand still. Surely Masonry, by its spirit and genius international, has a mission here, especially among peoples who have a common conception of civilization. Howbeit, for such a ministry we need what ultimately, or soon or late, we must have, some kind of Masonic world fellowship. No sovereignty need be surrendered, no jurisdiction invaded, no legislation enacted. But we must somehow make articulate and effective the spirit of unity, purpose and aspiration latent in universal Masonry, as an influence making for goodwill among men.

THE OPPORTUNITY FOR BROTHERHOOD

THE days in which we live may not be the best or the worst in history, but to us they are the most interesting. "The world is so full of a number of things, I am sure we should all be as happy as kings," said Stevenson. But we are not happy, and we are not kings. Whether we will or no, humanity is drawn together, jammed together, and we can never be happy until we learn to live together.

The outstanding trait of our times is an extreme complexity of life. What a variety of interests appeal to men, bombarding them from every side all the time. As a result there is a chaos of conflicting ideas, a widespread fermentation of mind, a lack of repose, and unstable equilibrium of thought and life. Over this tossing sea of activity and change, there hangs a cloudy apprehension of uncertainty —a cloud to some observers roseate with hope, to others dark with dread.

Consider the facts? For one thing, we have a vast and bewildering extension of the means of intercommunication. The railroad, the telegraph, the telephone, and now the radio make the earth a whispering gallery and a hall of mirrors. If a man wanted to be a hermit, there are only one or two places left on the globe which would suit his purpose. He might build his hut either at the North Pole or the South; but if he did so he would soon be joined by the agent of a land company seeking to establish a popular resort. There is hardly a spot left where the hum and rattle of the world does not beat upon the ear with more or less distinctness.

There is a like extension of the means of intelligence. Every man travels or talks with traveled men. The newspaper is omnipresent, and claims to be omniscient! Take the wings of the morning and and fly to the uttermost parts of the earth, and behold the morning paper flies on those same wings. Every part of the world knows about every other part; and the naked African prince who asked Stanley if the people of Europe talked much about him was a true son of his time. All the doings of the world, from the diplomatic fencings of the powers of Europe down to the heart-tragedies of the city slums, are but the gossip of an enlarged neighborhood. It is a noisy, snippy neighborhood, in which folk hang over the back fence and say nasty things about each other—but a neighborhood none the less.

Indeed, it looks as if the world is about to become too small and too familiar to afford sufficient stimulus to our jaded appetite for sensation, and men are foretelling the days when the space between the earth and Mars will be like the Straits of Dover, and the inhabitants of the neighboring planets will launch forth in electric air navies and fight for the supremacy of the solar system, using the Moon for a national cemetery!

The result of this shrinking of the earth has been

a rapid death of provincialism and the growth of the cosmopolitan spirit. Once local ideas were the standards by which men measured every thought and custom that chanced to stray from the outlying regions of darkness into the little circle of light which they inhabited. Every deviation from the manners and customs of the neighborhood, or the state, was deemed a violation of the order of the universe, an exhibition of anarchy, a bit of the original chaos not yet reduced to system.

By the sudden enlargement of the neighborhood to the limits of the world, the different and incongruous local ideals, customs and traditions have jostled each other in strange confusion. They have tended to neutralize and destroy one another, or at least have stripped one another of much of their authority and sacredness, until men are half ashamed to wear a lingering rag of local prejudice, and look with tolerant and pleased eye upon the variegated life of the race, and rejoice in the differences of custom, speech and ideas as adding infinitely to its picturesqueness and philosophic interest.

Today men pride themselves upon being citizens of the world. We are losing the power of being surprised. Goldsmith's "Citizen of the World," as he traveled into strange lands, remarked: "When I have ceased to wonder I may possible grow wise"; and surely, we have reached the point in our development when the wisdom ought to be in evidence. We are no longer shocked by strange customs, and discoveries which would have startled us fifty years ago hardly keep pace with our expectations. New ideas have become commonplace. Bernard Shaw finds himself an old fogey. The freshest ideas are the old ones, forgotten in the hurry of running after the novel.

The result of all this process, so hastily sketched, is a growing sense of the unity of humanity. The feeling of fraternity is one of the noblest notes of our times. It is atmospheric. It is insistent. It is passionate. It is the first article of the creed of the age. It is an article of the religion of every man; and is the only religion which many men have. Like other creeds, it is belied every day in practice; but it stirs the heart as nothing else. Even the most phlegmatic must respond to it in some degree, while sanguine idealists become ecstatic, dream dreams and see visions.

Such is the opportunity for brotherhood today. Once a fine sentiment, it has become a necessity— a vast inflowing tide of facts and the pressure of reality the might of which we can neither measure nor forever resist. But it must pass from sentiment to science, and the irritation we feel today, in the wake of the war, is due to the discovery of the fact that we are in truth brothers, to the last man of us, whether we like it or not. Perhaps the greatest truth burned into our minds by the World War is that the good of the race as a whole does actually exist, and that no one race or land can reach its full development by itself.

In such a world Freemasonry, the oldest and greatest fraternity known among men, must now do its work. Its secret is now the open secret and quest of the world. Its truth is the universal dogma. Its ideas and methods are copied in a thousand ways.

How will Masonry meet this marvelous age and measure up to its opportunity? Is it a progressive science, as it claims to be? Can Masonry itself unite in a common undertaking for the common good, in service to mankind?